8.50

Essay Index

NOVELISTS
We are Seven

NOVELISTS
We Are Seven

BY
PATRICK BRAYBROOKE

Essay Index

BOOKS FOR LIBRARIES PRESS
FREEPORT, NEW YORK

First Published 1926
Reprinted in this Series 1966, 1969

STANDARD BOOK NUMBER:
8369-1320-5

LIBRARY OF CONGRESS CATALOG CARD NUMBER:
67-22075

PRINTED IN THE UNITED STATES OF AMERICA

AUTHOR'S PREFACE

This book concerns seven of the leading novelists of to-day. Each novelist is worth a book, but in a short Essay I have attempted to give some idea of the "Essence" of each writer making up this company of Seven.

PATRICK BRAYBROOKE.

1 Leinster Square, Hyde Park.
Spring, 1926.

CONTENTS

PORTRAIT NUMBER ONE
TEMPLE THURSTON

PORTRAIT NUMBER ONE

TEMPLE THURSTON

I BELIEVE that I am perfectly right when I insist that a great deal of Mr. Thurston's astonishingly brilliant work has to do with the philosophy of womanhood. And perhaps a great romantic novelist, as Mr. Thurston is, must be logically expected to have a great deal to say about women. For, say what you like about the emancipation of woman, even if you admit that this emancipation is but a subtle form of slavery, novelists must concern themselves very largely with the aspects of the feminine mind. Women probably read novels much more than men for two reasons. The one that on the whole they are less intelligent than men, the other that they are infinitely more romantic.

Now the clever novelist, and Mr. Thurston is in every way possessed of that delightful appellation, knows perfectly well that women like to read about themselves, especially when the writings are by a man. But I would not for one instant suggest that Mr. Thurston merely writes much of women for any commercial motive such as good selling. In his work I find a very sincere and sympathetic wish to understand the feminine mind, that mind which perhaps really keeps the world from dying of a blatant despair.

11

For the attempt by the novelist to know of the feminine mind is in its essence a noble endeavour. It is a noble endeavour because it displays an inherent unselfishness, a wish to discover the other point of view, a wish that woman shall occupy her proper place in the universe. I do not wish to be misunderstood when I say that Mr. Thurston deals with commonplace women, I do not wish to imply that therefore his women are not worthy of much consideration. It is true that the commonplace woman has but little to distinguish her, her name is unknown, her life passes in absolute obscurity. But for the novelist, it is the commonplace woman who is the interpreter of her sex, of the ambitions of her sex. Mr. Thurston then deals with commonplace women for the obviously good reason that he wishes to construct a non-academic philosophy of womanhood. And you do not get the philosophy of woman by studying all her mental states and all her racial properties and propensities, you get her philosophy by observing her when she is doing such ordinary things as talking to children or making toast over the sitting-room fire. Wherefore let it be said that Mr. Thurston " catches " woman in her most ordinary moments. It will be well worth our while to spend some time in an examination of the subtle touches which convince me that Mr. Thurston does know an enormous amount about that extraordinary bit of Divinity, the ordinary woman. Those ordinary women who pass through life absolutely unknown, except to a small circle, yet when they pass away, leave behind a small circle which never but bitterly regrets the " passing."

So we will let Mr. Thurston interpret something of woman for us and he shall do so by a consideration of what he says in some of his beautiful novels. For Mr.

TEMPLE THURSTON

Thurston is a beautiful writer, and he is a beautiful writer because he is a kind and sympathetic writer, because he can write of " beautiful nonsense " and let us know that this " beautiful nonsense " concerns a city and perhaps the city is on so high a hill that it is just out of sight.

Though I know full well that Mr. Thurston will not agree with me, though I know that I shall evoke his displeasure, I say with all the strength that I can that his " City of Beautiful Nonsense " is a wonderful book and a thing of pure and undefiled beauty.

And therefore, because I love this " City of Beautiful Nonsense," because I love its sweet impossibility, because I love the homeliness of Kensington Gardens and the desperate wonder of Venice, because I love the romantic meeting of the man and the woman who met under the kindly gaze of Saint Joseph, because I love the divine melancholy of the book, because I love all these things, I take much of my matter concerning the women of Mr. Thurston from this great romantic novel.

I do not know in all Mr. Thurston's writings a more delicious piece of romance than the visit that Jill made to John on that dreadfully dull Easter Sunday. I say dull, because in " The City of Beautiful Nonsense " John expected to spend that Sunday all alone and a Sunday all alone in London is an experience of blank misery. So when Jill arrives quite unexpectedly to see John, we find that Mr. Thurston knows exactly how a woman feels when she pays an unexpected visit, especially when that visit is somewhat unconventional, in the sense that cowards and pious hypocrites have made these sex conventions, lest nature should assert its most natural rights.

Mr. Thurston, most admirably, describes how Jill is not quite sure whether John is glad to see her.

" ' I came,' said she, ' on chance.   Aren't you glad to
see me ?'

" There was just that fraction's pause before he replied—that pause into which a woman's mind leaps for
an answer.   And how accurately she makes that leap,
how surely she reaches the mental ground upon which
you take your place, you will never be able truly to
appreciate."

This is just where Mr. Thurston gets *nearly* at the right
consideration of the feminine mind.   But not quite.   A
woman once she is determined to be unconventional is
absolutely thorough going, but one thing will beat her.
That is if she feels she is giving herself where she is not
wanted.   Mr. Thurston does not quite seem to go far
enough in this matter.   He rightly insists that Jill wants
to know that John is glad to see her, but he does not
follow the reasoning out to its logical conclusion, that what
Jill wants to be perfectly certain of, is that she is not
putting herself in a false position for someone who does
not care as much as she thought he would.

But if I am right in suggesting that in this particular
passage Mr. Thurston only gets at three-quarters of the
reason of Jill's question, a few lines later we get an absolutely true picture of a feminine characteristic.

" She seated herself easily in the chair to which she
was accustomed.   She began drawing the pins out of
her hat, as a woman does when she feels at home."

This is absolutely true.   Love may end in a very close
parallel to lust but love begins when a woman takes her
hat off and does so without considering the action.   For

you see perhaps the first thing a woman does when she
arrives at her home after the honeymoon, is to take the
pins out of her hat, and women when they are in love
think a long way ahead.

.   .   .   .

Two more thoughts and I must leave my city of beautiful nonsense for there is much that must be written of
Mr. Thurston and alas, it cannot all be found in his
nonsense city. One thought is about snobs, those feminine snobs whose environment is the universe, and whose
soul is a putrid excrescence, that infects all who come in
contact with it.

Jill explains how her mother could not receive John
until she knew where he lived. The essence of that
snobbery which has made it necessary that the hottest
part of Hell should be reserved for the souls of snobbish
women, who have lived as snobs and died as snobs, and
taken their place where the worms devour their miserable
bodies.

   "'She said, of course, that it was impossible for me
to know you until you had come properly as a visitor
to the house, and that she couldn't ask you until she
knew where you lived.'"

One last thought from my lovely city. It shall be of
that morning when all is the same outside, but in the room
a cold, still white body lies, so still that it will never
move again. Look out of the window, the street is the
same, the people still rush carelessly by, the sun is beginning to shine, the shops are making ready for the buyers
who will buy that they may live, but on the bed is a form

that will never move until others bear it away, for in the night messengers have been and we who have not seen their entrance, are desolately aware that we are for ever alone.   Mr. Thurston's description of such an early morning in the city of Venice is a piece of brilliant description.

> " At her accustomed hour of the morning, came Claudina into the little room.   Feeling her way to the window, she threw open wide the jalousies.   A flood of sunshine beat into the room and made all dazzling white.   She turned to the bed.   There was the still white head alone upon the pillow, the powerless hand just showing from beneath the coverlet still holding tightly its string of beads.
> " '*Buon giorno, signora,*' she said, trying to make the note of some cheerfulness in her voice.
> " But there was no reply.
> " Far away out in the wonderful city, she heard the cry of a gondolier.   ' Ohe '—and in through the window, there floated a butterfly of white that had been beating its wings against the jalousies outside.   Into the room it flew, dipping and dancing, swaying and lifting in the free air of the day just born."

   .   .   .   .

Before passing on to discuss certain other of the characteristics of Mr. Thurston's work, it will be interesting to say a little more about his philosophy of womanhood. There is, in " The Garden of Resurrection," a rather charming little passage about the certain affinity women have to children.   The reason why women like pretty frocks and pretty hats is not entirely a matter of sex appeal, it is much more simple than that. It is that women are like children, they love that which has plenty of colour, that which pleases the eye. Of course, there are certain women who prefer scholarship and matters of politics to hats and frocks, but these are not really women, they are either, university masculine " women " or embittered spinsters. But Mr. Thurston always writes of women as they really are, that is, beings not too serious, not too grown up, not too human, not too divine. The passage which has evoked these thoughts deals with how women like, not only pretty hats and frocks but a big plateful of cakes and plenty to choose. The passage is written with all that charm and delicate understanding of which Mr. Thurston is so eminently possessed.

> " It pleases them also to know that there is a lot to choose from. They love being unable to make up their minds amidst a galaxy of riches. They like you to select for them, just so that they may realise how your selection has eliminated the very thing they did not want."

But one more example of Mr. Thurston's thoughts about women and I must turn to something else. It is of that almost insolent sneer that many men make, that religion, by which I mean the mechanical rites of it, appeals to women. In " The Greatest Wish in the World " Mr. Thurston goes very deeply into this question of women and their love for religion. It is perhaps almost a matter of sex, a matter of loving. The passage is well worth quoting because it shows Mr. Thurston to be a deep thinker as well as a brilliant novelist, which combination readily tells us the secret of his fine and pure genius.

" It is when she rises from her knees in prayer that a
woman is most easily won to love. It is when she is
first thrilled by the whisperings of passion that you
will find her most ready to fall upon her knees and
pray."

Then Mr. Thurston tells us why Christianity is the religion of women and he is so perfectly right that perhaps
Christ meant His religion to be for women, not that men
should leave it on one side, but rather that they might
learn it at their mother's knees, so that the learning should
be made through the most perfect of human channels.

" It is by reason of this, that Christianity is the
religion of women. They understand what it means to
love Christ. A man can only fear God, and that is
most times so derogatory to his dignity that he would
as lief go without a religion at all."

Perhaps then I have made it clear that Mr. Thurston
does try very hard to see the feminine point of view and
I suggest most earnestly that to a very large extent he
succeeds in his ambition.

.   .   .   .

Being in every way a master of the art of writing in a
charming manner, it follows almost naturally, that Mr.
Thurston should be a master of the divine art of the
writing of tragedy. For tragedy is a most hopeful thing,
it is one of those contingencies that proves the fact of
immortality. The man or woman who commits suicide
depicts and postulates that life is unending, for I take it,
that the suicide who wishes to get out of this life, infers

(muddled though his brain may be) that he will get into some *better* existence. Whether he does or not is a mute question, the fact remains that life must continue, the pistol shot or the despairing plunge into the river or the fatal dose of poison, all these cannot release the life force which has kept the body, into a state of nothingness. Now tragedy is likely to appeal to a romantic writer (and Mr. Thurston is this delightful thing), because the mind of a really considerable thinker, moves in opposing forces. If London can be a beautiful city full of childish nonsense, if it can show the glory of unconventional love sitting on two penny chairs in Kensington Gardens, if it can show the beauty of religion in a little half-lit Catholic chapel, London can show the other side. London can show the hateful cruelty of its streets, it can show the abominations of the lust of millions, it can show the painted street woman sneaking along with one eye on a policeman, and the other on the young fool from the country or the more sophisticated fool in top hat and " boiled shirt."

All this has a great deal to do with Mr. Thurston because he writes of two London's, one in " The City of Beautiful Nonsense," the other in " Sally Bishop." " Sally Bishop " is a tragedy because superior people think it is a comedy. Very superior people who know more about the Holy Communion than did the Disciples at The Last Supper, are no doubt faintly amused that a clergyman should get drunk on Consecrated wine. But less superior people with a good deal more intelligence than the more superior people, can see that such a contingency is a dire tragedy, not because the clergyman got drunk, but because of the absurd idea of certain Church people that no Consecrated wine must be left. And really if they think this, they are in the position of suggesting that the

Founder of the Christian form of Eucharist was lacking
in common sense, a subtle way of expressing blasphemy.
And I rather think that Mr. Thurston is a little angry
when he tells us of the downfall of Sally's father, he is a
little angry that a clergyman should be bound to either
get drunk or offend his unintelligent congregation by
leaving a little Consecrated wine.   However, this unfortunate difficulty which Mr. Bishop experienced allows
Mr. Thurston to write a very calm and realistic story of a
girl whose only really happy moment in London, was when
she committed suicide or *after* she had committed suicide.

There is in the very middle of the drama of Sally Bishop
a tense little bit of dialogue concerning the pathos of the
unsuccessful prostitute.   The unsuccessful prostitute is
a miserable figure, but not so miserable as the unsuccessful
priest.   The unsuccessful prostitute only deals with
bodies, but the unsuccessful priest deals with souls.   Mr.
Thurston quite obviously knows a great deal about the
dialogue of the women of the streets and it is a fine piece
of his courage that he is not afraid to make this knowledge
widespread.   When it is recognised that prostitutes are
serious people who consider their particular work in particular ways, we shall perhaps do something to understand
them, and provide for them something more attractive
than the sudden austerity of well meaning rescue workers.
This following piece of dialogue might be heard any evening in that whirlpool of inanity and artificiality, Piccadilly Circus.

> " 'I pray God no man 'll offer me ten bob to-night,'
> she had said to another woman.
> " 'Why ?
> " 'Why ? Gosh ! I'd take it.' "

When Mr. Thurston can write like this, he is a very sincere artist and his sincerity is obviously fearless and perfectly spontaneous.

Towards the end of the tragedy when Sally is getting near to her last days, there is a very remarkable bit of dialogue, when Sally desires that she shall be the recipient of a child and the father of the child shall be Traill. It is a fine piece of understanding ; for some women are so fond of children that they have no wish for any man, beyond that he shall be the necessary instrument for the fulfilling of the maternal wish. A woman when she really desires a child is perfectly unscrupulous, while a man never by any chance wants an illegitimate child, for the very simple reason that he has no idea what to do with it, and convention with its usual muddle headedness has determined that children born out of wedlock are a disgrace. Mr. Thurston deals with a difficult situation in a brilliant manner, and let it be said in passing that perhaps Mr. Thurston is one of the best writers of dialogue among living novelists. And this is no mean achievement when dialogue to-day is so surprisingly good and also delicate. I will give a little of the dialogue between Traill and Sally on the question of her wished for maternity and his determination that no illegitimate child shall be his.

"'Then help me not to be lonely now,' she begged. She could see the wave of repulsion beat across his face, but even that could not deter her 'Oh, I don't mean that you should come back and live with me,' she went on. 'It isn't for that. You can't, you surely can't hate me as much as all that.' It was not in her knowledge to realise that he must love her, greater than he had ever loved, if she were to win. To the

woman needing the child it is the child alone ; to the
man the child is only the child when it is his."

So we get the admirable reply to the request.   It brings
out very clearly the fundamental difference in point of
view between the man and the woman.   And it also shows
very clearly that Mr. Thurston is a very deep student of
human nature and one whose judgment is worth very
serious consideration.   It cannot be said that all novelists,
(who have even attained to eminence), are worth much
more than mere passing interest, but Mr. Thurston uses
his art to instruct as well as amuse.   And the combination is very useful and merits much praise.   Thus Traill
replies to poor Sally, poor Sally who after all is but being
as true to her nature, as the perfectly pure girl who is
true to *her* nature and gets her child after the delicious
sanctity and hypocrisy of the average marriage.

    " 'I don't hate you,' he said.   He picked up his hat
from the settee and her heart dropped to a leaden
weight.   ' You seem to harp on that.   But what you
ask, you surely must realise is frankly impossible.   I
don't wish to be responsible for a child.'"

Mr. Thurston makes Sally utter yet one more plea.   It is
admirable psychology, for women know that men do not
like being responsible for the unpleasing results of their
so-called illegal unions.   But Traill is true to his own
nature, he will live with a woman, get tired of her and
then be quite ashamed at the preposterous idea of being
responsible for a child.   Men are moral when they wish
to be, but women are perfectly willing to risk morality

when maternity is wished, which really shows that women are cleverer than moralists.

Here is poor Sally's plea.

"'You needn't be responsible,' she said, eagerly."

To which Traill replies, shuffling, with true masculine genius.

"'If I did have a child, I should want to see it.'"

But it must be added that many men wish more than anything that they may not see the child that is their's ; for pockets and illegitimacy have a disagreeable parallelism.

Once a man is tired of a woman, nothing will bring him back, fear, pity, anger, nothing can restore that sense of extreme comradeship which makes men and women live together and defy the marriage laws. Admirably does Mr. Thurston bring out this by the passages I have quoted.

With enormous commonsense Mr. Thurston brings "Sally Bishop" to the inevitable conclusion. The happiest ending for a woman who is deserted by her lover is that she should commit suicide, it is a far less punishment than that she be tolerated for the rest of her life by a number of highly moral women who have been too unattractive to be anything but possessed of meritorious virtue. The ending of Sally is on a dramatic note, no miserable limp body dragged from the Thames, but a finding of her by Traill, so that he should lift her dead body as so often he had lifted her live body, when it was full of that girlish life which seems at the time an everlasting mode of activity. Mr. Thurston says just

enough and not too much, life does end and the beholders
can do no more than suggest that Sally has passed from
misery to something better. It is a form of popular
sentiment that has perhaps more truth in it, than we,
who would reduce everything to proof, imagine.

> " With a muffled sound, Traill forced himself to
> her side. He put his arm round her. He lifted her up.
> The body dragged against him, the head swung from
> the loose neck.
>   " ' Sally's had her bad time,' said Janet, hoarsely,
> ' and my God it's over now.' "

.   .   .   .

I have already said that Mr. Thurston is a master of
charm and a master of tragedy. He is also a master of
detail or rather getting at the essence of a character by
means of penetrating glimpses. Perhaps he uses what
may be called the " glimpse " method of letting us know
what type of person he is writing about. The day is for
the present past when novelists wrote long cumbersome
descriptions of characters with the melancholy result
that the reader had no conceivable idea of what sort of
person the character really was. Mr. Thurston has an
uncanny way of digging out the reality of the character he
is drawing and he does this almost as it were in parenthesis.

It is of course the best way of depicting a person. We
only really know the outlook of someone else by their
little actions, by these minute actions we are enabled to
see something of the actual mind behind. In " Richard
Furlong " there is a delightful touch, concerning a landlady, those people who are commonly thought as grasping
and slightly fat and untidy. Mr. Thurston reveals by

one little aside, the real woman beneath the landlady
with whom Furlong made his home in London, that city
which, like all fools, he thought would necessarily help his
art.   Furlong has been told by a newspaper man that his
drawings are no good.   Perhaps more hearts are broken
and ambitions crushed in Editorial offices than anywhere,
yet also in these inhuman abodes reputations get their
first impetus.   Furlong has gone back to his lodgings in
that state of despair when everything is of the blackest.
blackness.   The landlady tries to comfort him and it is
here that we get one of the masterly touches of Mr.
Thurston.

> " She took his arm and in the midst of this mono-
> tonous business of the oil shop, suddenly felt a mother
> again.
> " ' I'll come presently,' he said. ' I'll come presently.'
> " She chose the wisest course and left him.   Down-
> stairs in the parlour she laid out the tea for three.
> " ' Nice boy that,' she continually muttered to her-
> self, ' nice boy that.'
> " And it was all because he had made her feel a
> mother again."

Mr. Thurston has a very sure understanding of human
nature and it is by these little comments that he shows us
what a fine thing human nature is at bedrock.

Being a very close and observant watcher of life, it
follows almost naturally that much of Mr. Thurston's
writing is sad.   The novelist who observes with that close
scrutiny which produces the successful fiction writer must
be aware that taken all together life is sad.   The very fact
that many people are intensely gay illustrates the un-

doubted fact that the essence of life is sad. The reason
that people dance, make merry, shout and sing is not
that they are happy, but that they wish to escape from
thought, for nearly all thought is in reality a sad thing.
The sadness of Mr. Thurston is on the whole something
that is attractive, it is a gentle sadness, a sadness that
love passes, a sadness that those who we would most keep
slip quietly away, a sadness that has something of peace,
a sadness that has something akin to angry restlessness.
There is in Mr. Thurston's work the sadness of cities, the
sadness of frustrated ambition, the sadness of the pitiless
cruelty of man to man, woman to woman, man to woman,
woman to man.

Yet behind all perhaps there is something of the childlike outlook in Mr. Thurston's work, people are pleased
with small things, with transitory joys, yet withal they
are petulant, unsatisfied and intensely restless.

It is not easy to say what is the religious significance
of Mr. Thurston's work. There is a certain liking for the
Catholic religion, not so much for what it teaches as the
way it appeals to man's love for the ornate and the romantic. For the Catholic religion, whether it be true or
false or a little true and a little false, is a thing of pure
beauty, even if it is only regarded from the purely sen-
suous point of view. And perhaps because Mr. Thurston
does so philosophise about women is a reason why there
should be in his work much concerning the Catholic religion. Say what you like of the Catholic religion, that it is
the most splendidly true inheritance that man can possess
or say that it is full of the grossest error, the fact remains
that this religion is intimately bound up with women. It
does not in the least matter whether The Virgin was an exceptional woman who produced an exceptional child in an

exceptional manner, or whether she was a very ordinary Jewish mother who happened to be selected for playing a unique part in history, it is certain that a novelist who writes a good deal of women and also a good deal of religion will be unable to leave on one side that religion which truly or falsely exalts above all, a Jewish woman who might be or might not be, The Mother of God.

Let me show Mr. Thurston a master of yet one other art of writing. That is, in the curious form of art that is known as description. Description may well vary between the exaggerated sensationalism of the newspaper reporter and the wondrous intimate pictures of great literary artists. I give one example of the power of writing description that is possessed by Mr. Thurston. And it shall be of Venice.

" Come to Venice in the early morning and you will see a city bathed in a sea of light ; for it is not only the sun that shines upon it, but that, like the white shoulders of a mermaid glittering with the water drops as she rises out of the sea, this wonderful city is not illuminated only, but is drenched in light itself. Come to Venice in the early morning and you will see a smelter's furnace into which has been cast the gold and silver from a boundless treasure hoard. You will see all that white and yellow metal running in molten streams of light ; you will see the vibrating waves of air as the flames leap upward, curling and twisting to the very gates of heaven itself. You will see a city of gold and silver, of light and air, all made liquid in one sea of brilliance, if you do but come to Venice in the early morning."

This is surely a wonderful description, perhaps something like what we still believe Heaven is.

I suppose in the ordinary sense of the word Mr. Thurston would be called a popular novelist. But he is evidently something more. He is a serious novelist. His seriousness is never forced, it is even so hidden in the charm of his writings that its note may be missed.

" Sally Bishop " is a serious novel for it shows that life for a girl in a great city can quite easily lead to a premature death in that same city. Mr. Thurston, if all his utterances be taken together, has most undoubtedly composed a philosophy of womanhood. That it has value seems to me to be perfectly certain. Perhaps the essence of his philosophy of woman is that she is a little childlike and usually lovable.

It may of course be urged with a good deal of truth that much of Mr. Thurston's work is sentimental. But if it is, it is a very excellent thing that this should be so. A little more sentiment in the modern world would do much to make the world less hard and disagreeable. And if Mr. Thurston is sentimental it is because he deals with sentimental subjects. Who could write of a city of beautiful nonsense and not be in the best sense sentimental ? Who could write of a young man who comes like Dick Whittington to London to try his fortune and not be sentimental ? Who could write the love story of an ugly man and not be sentimental ? Certainly not Mr. Thurston, who always writes with an abounding sympathy. And why should it be brought almost as a charge, that a novelist is sentimental ? It is because we have lost the real worth of life. It is because we prefer the glare of the streets to the pale grandeur of the moon, it is because we prefer the rustle of money to the half hidden lights near the Altar, it is because we prefer to sneer at the romances of young people rather than to praise their delicious purity, it is because we prefer to build houses to man rather than to raise temples to the divine.

Mr. Thurston sees life as a beautiful thing, he also sees it as something execrable, but behind all there is a plea that life can be so charming, so white, it can shine like the summer sun, it can move easily and leave behind a feeling of rest and content.

The people that Mr. Thurston writes of are in every way undistinguished, they would be those we pass in the street, those who play the small parts in the world's affairs, those whose names are as unknown as the multitudes who lie so thick in hundreds of quiet churchyards. And it is because Mr. Thurston writes of commonplace men and commonplace women, that he writes of Life, for Life is not seen through those who attain eminence, but rather through those who are merely cogs in the great wheel. Mr. Thurston is the novelist who writes of the joys and sorrows of the man and woman in the next house, he can make us laugh at their jokes, he can make us weep at their sorrows, he can make us angry at their follies but he can make us see, even though it be faintly, something of the inherent grandeur of human life. Mr. Thurston gives the impression of being a watcher of life, a man who ponders.

. . . .

It is no part of this book to deal with any of the plays of Mr. Thurston and therefore it is not necessary to say more than that much of his dramatic work is of a very high order.

In his novels, Mr. Thurston touches much on the sadness and charm of love. His books probably are more likely to appeal to women than to men. He has great powers of description, his books read with that ease that can only be produced by a gifted writer of fiction. As I have said, a serious note runs through Mr. Thurston's work. He teaches that life is an interesting thing, though hard. On the whole I think it is fair to say that he considers life harder for a woman than for a man. Man is callous, unscrupulous and woman suffers. Woman is kind, gentle, yet willing to be immoral in the search for love and maternity.

In a word, Mr. Thurston is a very pleasant teller of a story, the careful delineator of character and a master of creating romance. To-day Mr. Thurston lives away down in Kent in an old world house that almost scornfully regards the motors that rush by outside. Down in this fair garden of England Mr. Thurston writes much and in as much seclusion as a famous man can ever be, pursues the noble task of making fiction, that those whose lives are very dull, may read and take courage again.

Although an admirable host, Mr. Thurston does not mix much with the outside world. He has probably too much of his own literary work to be able to afford the necessary time and loss of energy that result from mixing with mortals.

If one would have converse with those immortals who guide the pens of ready writers, it is almost a necessary corollary that mortals must not be allowed to intrude too often. Mr. Thurston displays in all his books a knowledge of people and perhaps by a process of pondering and the intercourse with a limited number of people, he is enabled to gain this knowledge and put it in his books. Whatever may be the reward of his work to himself, his books have a sure place, for they amuse and instruct and at the same time appeal to that romantic part of a person, which is always there, if only it can be discovered.

END OF PORTRAIT ONE

PORTRAIT NUMBER TWO
MAY SINCLAIR

PORTRAIT NUMBER TWO

MAY SINCLAIR

I IMAGINE that anybody who endeavoured to write something about a distinguished novelist, in the space of a few thousand words, would be aware that much of what he would like to say would have to be left on one side. A person who writes of a novelist in such a manner as is attempted in this book, has perhaps two courses open to him. On the one hand he may write of the general position of the novelist, on the other he may write *something* of the general position of the novelist and at the same time concentrate on some particular point in the particular novelist's work. In this essay on Miss Sinclair, I propose to adopt the second course and I propose further to consider a particular point of her work at once. This is with regard to her drawing of a clergyman. The matter is so important that I have no hesitation in devoting the greater part of this Essay to an examination of the work of Miss Sinclair with regard to the drawing of an English clergyman.

.   .   .   .

It is a fact that the clergyman is the most important person in the world. He is of far more consequence than the Governor of the Bank of England and even of

more consequence than a popular actress! It is vitally
of consequence whether the clergyman is right in what he
says. It is of much more vital consequence if he is
wrong in what he says. I have determined to indulge
in a lengthy digression and say something about the
popular misconceptions regarding clergymen. The digression is in no way out of place as it will lead me up to the
special consideration of this essay, the clergyman that
Miss Sinclair draws in " A Cure of Souls."

There are a great many people who with great nonsense
pronounce that clergymen are a type. You have only
to enter the average drawing room of the average English
middle class person to hear it said, that that particular
man is a typical clergyman. This is of course as great
nonsense as saying that that particular dustman is a
typical dustman or that that particular butcher is a
typical butcher. The probable reason that the clergy
are looked upon so much as a type, is that a very large
proportion of them dress in the same manner. But such
an argument (and I believe it is a cause of suggesting the
clergy to be of a type), is a perfectly ridiculous one. It is
as ridiculous as saying that all private soldiers are alike
because, on parade, they have polished buttons and all
stand in precisely the same way at precisely the same
moment.

Very well then ; public opinion with its usual policy
of being delightfully wrong and futile pronounces that
there is a type clergyman, mainly I suggest because
many of them wear the same dress. On the other hand
the deduction made by the public may emanate from the
fact that many clergymen who pass along the public
streets pat small children on the head. At any rate the
clergy are *not* a type any more than dustmen are a type

or postmen are a type or authors are a type. Therefore
when it is said that Mr. X is a typical clergyman what is
implied is that there are ten thousand other clergymen
like Mr. X. Whereas the truth of the matter is, that there
are no other clergymen like Mr. X, for a clergyman is a
member of humanity and humanity is intensely individual.
And yet in saying anything about Miss Sinclair's drawing
of a clergyman I am almost bound to utter a fallacy. For
I am almost bound to ask whether Canon Chamberlain
is a well-drawn clergyman and to do this, it is almost
necessary to ask whether he is typical, the very word that
I have objected to as being an absurdity. But I need
not mean what popular opinion means by saying that a
clergyman is typical. What I do mean is that; can
Canon Chamberlain be found in real life ? I do not wish
to discuss whether Canon Chamberlain is typical because
I am convinced that there are no such people as typical
people. What I want to discuss is the *reality* of Canon
Chamberlain. But before I do this I shall again digress.
I have already suggested and I am quite convinced that I
am more right than wrong, that public opinion has been
wrong in attaching so frequently the word typical to a
clergyman. My second digression, which is leading me yet
nearer to Miss Sinclair, is to ask what has fiction done in
the matter of creating clergymen. It has very largely
fallen in line with public opinion. It has not so much
created a " typical " clergyman, it has, instead, with great
obstinacy generally speaking divided the clergy into two
classes. It has made the clergyman a saint, on the other
hand it has made him a poor kind of humbug. And it is
pretty safe to say that both contentions are equally wrong.
Most clergymen are not saints, for the very good reason
that they have not the intelligence to be such, most

clergymen are not humbugs because they are too intelligent to be so.

Fiction in dealing with a clergyman has for the most part been extremely cowardly. It has either pandered to those whose feeble intelligence loves to be satiated by the sickly saintliness of fiction clergymen or it has pandered to those whose equally feeble intelligence has desired to be fed on the clergyman who is a humbug. The question of reality, the most important question of all, has seldom been considered. Only let a clergyman be drawn to please the reader and nothing else has mattered, and it is a curious fact that those who like to read of the clergy as saints, also like to read of them as rogues. But the converse is probably untrue.

.   .   .   , ...

It is peculiarly appropriate that a woman should write of a clergyman. For the fact of a woman writing of a clergyman leads to an interesting consideration respecting the modern woman. The last few years has seen a distinct reversal in feminine opinion concerning the clergy. Not long ago it was thought, and there was good reason for the thought, that women as a whole were on the side of the clergy. At the present day intellectual womanhood is certainly not, for the most part, anything but hostile to the clergy. There is a feeling of contempt for them, they are thought to be reactionary. Women who to-day demand divorce, are naturally annoyed at the obstinacy of the clergy. The modern woman is inclined to be irritated by the clergy who demand that that which is old, permanent, is best. It is no part of this book to say whether woman or rather intellectual woman (for the average woman's opinion is of no consequence whatever), is right in her attitude of hostility to the clergy. Miss

MAY SINCLAIR

Sinclair is one of the best of the intellectual women writers of the present day. To a certain extent she has been a pioneer, a pioneer in the art of writing profoundly introspective novels. It is then of vast interest and also of vast worth to examine the portrait that Miss Sinclair draws of a clergyman.

There is probably no class of persons so liable to attack as the clergy. Their calling quite naturally renders them liable to hostility, ridicule. The clergyman however well he may do his work, however conscientious he may be, must by his very ethical code be unpopular with the vast majority of those people who prefer to pander to the flesh, who prefer to taste the delights of Earth rather than put them on one side, for the very doubtful promises of Heaven. Now it is no good denying that Miss Sinclair in her marvellously fine book " A Cure of Souls " is hostile to the clergy. She is not exactly contemptuous, rather she dissects them and finds them to be full of the usual human failings. In as far as she does this, Miss Sinclair falls into a popular error. That is that the average clergyman should be wholly good, free from all pettiness and possessed of all the virtues. But that Miss Sinclair falls into this popular error, makes no difference to the fact that in Canon Chamberlain, we have a most careful study of an English clergyman. Without any further general discussion it will now be convenient to subject her book to a somewhat exhaustive examination. If it be said that I spend too much of my space on this one book, it is merely that out of a wealth of very exceptional work, Miss Sinclair in " A Cure of Souls " seems to me, to rise to her greatest height.

Very early on in her book, Miss Sinclair considers the question of what I shall call clerical snobbery. As I

have already insisted on, any idea that the clergy act in
what has been called a "typical" manner, is utterly
and abominably fallacious.   But it is an unfortunate
fact that snobbery is very rampant among the English
clergy.   No doubt this appalling condition of affairs is
due to the fact that the clergy rank as County people.

But Miss Sinclair goes much more deeply into the
question of clerical snobbery.   She is not content with
inferring that Canon Chamberlain liked having to do with
the well-to-do people in his parish, rather she says, and
says with very great emphasis, that the Canon was snobbish even in respect of taking funerals.   It is indeed a
sad thing when it can be truthfully said, (and it can be
truthfully said), that the clergy are so concerned with the
flesh that they will only administer the last rites to those
who have been important.   In fact, it is a probable fact
that many clergy would have endeavoured *not* to officiate
at the burial of Christ, for He was but a poor carpenter
and none above a curate should of course be employed
to bury Him.   Let me quote how Miss Sinclair shows
Canon Chamberlain to be of that odious kind of clergyman who lets his curates take the uninteresting funerals,
the funerals which are very dull, very commonplace, with
not even a very local and unintelligent reporter present to
give a little publicity and mention the " officiating clergyman."

In regard to this matter of taking the funerals of unimportant people, Miss Sinclair pens a very devastating
attack.

" The Rector's peace was deepened by the thought
that Jackman, not he, would be out there in the blazing
sun, without a hat, taking Trinder's funeral."

And then comes the heavy attack, and it is vastly heavier in that it is, unfortunately, so true.

" If Trinder had been an important parishioner he would have had to take it himself. Mercifully, important parishioners very seldom died."

But Miss Sinclair is fair for the most part. It must not be supposed that the Canon was entirely selfish. He was deliciously unselfish, like most of us, when the unselfishness gave no trouble. We will send any amount of good things to our poorer neighbours so long as the troublesome business of taking them does not divulge itself upon us. So Canon Chamberlain had not been entirely unmindful of poor old Trinder.

" He was sorry that Trinder was dead, and that he would never see him again slipping forward on his hard wooden chair, never hear his voice, strangled by the hawking rattling cough."

Again Canon Chamberlain's sorrow is so like the sorrow of most of us. We are sorry that the old man is dead, not so much because we really liked him, but we are melancholy that the chocolates he so liked will never have to be bought again. We are sad that the old lady, whom we saw but seldom, is dead. For in the corner in the little old room, that we visited twice a year, a smallish old chair stands so lonely by itself. So when the funeral bell rings, though he who passes has not come our way very often, we regret that never more shall we go into the little village shop and ask how the old man, who sits in the back parlour, has been the last week or so. Thus Miss Sin-

clair with acute discrimination depicts, how in a sense,
Canon Chamberlain is sorry that old Trinder is dead.
He is sorry that even at the Rectory, the old man's
death has made one thing, never to be done again.

" He had sent poor old Trinder all the soup he wanted.
You might say Trinder had been kept alive by the soup
he had sent him."

It so happens that many clergy suffer now and again
from loss of faith.   Certain curates feel that they are cut
off from God.   In such a dire emergency they, quite
naturally seek advice from their rectors.   In a very
brilliant part of her book, Miss Sinclair shows us Canon
Chamberlain endeavouring to deal with his curate Jackman, when that very lugubrious person is suffering from
those black spiritual patches which seem to dog the most
conscientious Christians.   It cannot be said that Canon
Chamberlain says much that is of much good, but he is
not to be blamed.   If a man, whether he be curate or a
mere layman, loses God, it takes more than a mere Canon
to find Him again.   The discussion between Canon Chamberlain and his curate Jackman is so delicious, so astound-
ingly clever, so obviously true, that I shall give some
extracts from it.   Miss Sinclair is clever enough to let
us know, that what really worried Canon Chamberlain,
was not that Jackman had lost God, but rather that the
crumpets that the Canon loved were being wasted on the
unfortunate curate.
It may be interesting to suggest that the man who
thinks he has lost God need not be unduly alarmed.   In
fact it is highly probable that the Almighty has not
troubled much that an insignificant curate has lost Him.

On the other hand if the Almighty is really Absolute and
as interested in a flea as in a curate or Archbishop, it does
not matter to the individual that he feels he has lost God,
as naturally if God is Absolute and interested in all His
beings, then there can be no such thing as being lost to
God. But of course the individual may go through a
bad time, if he feels he has lost God, even if the feeling
is a painful delusion. So, many clergy, intensely conscious of how important they are to God, intensely conscious of how the working out of God's plan depends
upon them, sometimes feel that they have lost God and
no doubt imagine how melancholy the Almighty must be
at such a state of affairs. But few clergy, or laymen
either, see how colossal is the conceit that infers God is
lost, for it infers that the losing is not only detrimental
to the individual but detrimental to God as well.

So the background of the delightful loss of faith episode
is the Canon's drawing-room, with the accessories of
crumpets and hot tea.

Thus poor Jackman hurls the bombshell.

> "'It is that I do not, I cannot, believe any longer in
> God—in the existence of God.'"

This is disturbing to Canon Chamberlain, not so much
because of the theological catastrophe, but rather that
it should occur at tea-time. It is the small things that
irritate. God can care for Himself, but our hot crumpets
must not be allowed to become cold and greasy.

> " The Rector left off eating crumpet. He had not
> anticipated anything so serious as this. It might lead
> them anywhere. Into metaphysical abysses. And

why choose tea-time ?   It was too bad of Jackman.
Here was he, tired, wanting nothing but to be left to
finish his tea in peace, and there was Jackman, huddled
in his chair in an attitude of unimaginable discomfort
and saying that he didn't believe in God."

In trying to convince Jackman that the loss of God has
a good deal to do with health, Miss Sinclair makes Canon
Chamberlain say a very wise thing.   He infers that God
may be found by eating fruit.   If Eve and Adam lost God
by eating fruit, it is pretty obvious that many recover
God by eating fruit.   Most women when they have lost
God find him again by the simple means of discovering
a lover.   Most curates probably lose God because in the
first place they lose their health and quite unfairly put
the blame on " Evidences."

   " ' You should look after your health more carefully
than I think you do.   If you were to eat fresh fruit now,
every morning before breakfast any fresh fruit—you'd
be a better man, and these difficulties would pass out
of your mind as if they had never been.' "

But Mr. Jackman is not convinced and merely thinks
that the Canon is making fun of him.   It is a brilliant
piece of psychology on the part of Miss Sinclair.   Lose
your sense of humour and the ability to see that the right
understanding of theology depends more on daily habits
than profound metaphysics, and God is indeed for the
time being lost.   Thus Jackman replies with a bitter
idea that the Canon is minimising his deplorable state.

   " ' You think ' said Mr. Jackman with a sudden

dreadful humour, ' I should find God if I ate fresh fruit ' " ?

And the Canon, being a sensible man, as most selfish people really are, replies :

" ' I think that very probably you would find God. Especially if you left off looking for him.' "

Which is exactly why the most pious seekers after God are usually the most sensible that God is far off.

The whole rather melancholy discussion between the Canon and his curate ends as only such a discussion could end. Miss Sinclair with considerable discernment makes it perfectly apparent that all Canon Chamberlain really cares about, is that his curate shall get out. As to whether he finds God again or not, it is quite certain, that the Canon has no care whatever. In which Canon Chamberlain is extremely like many people, whose only concern for the spiritual difficulties of others, is to suggest something that will free them from irritating people. For the man who has lost money is an irritating person, the woman who has lost her lover is an abomination, but the curate who has lost God is an abomination of abominations ! Canon Chamberlain, always outwardly polite, ends the discussion in the quotation that I give.

" ' Well, don't do anything hastily. But, remember the ultimate decision rests with you.' "

And here Miss Sinclair adds a kind of mental note. For she knows the Canon only too well and she knows that like most Canons this one is anxious to visit a very

charming widow.   For when there is a charming widow
to be visited, what does it matter that an unimportant
curate has lost the Deity ?

" Which was as much as to say ' For goodness' sake
don't come worrying me about it again.'   He looked
at the clock.   He had just time to get to Kempsey
Maisey by half-past six."   .

Miss Sinclair has written this discussion with a great
deal of sincerity.   There is no fault that can be found
with the episode.   She has understood the point of view
of the worrying and unhealthy curate.   She has understood the attitude of the suave and contented canon.
And the unfortunate part of the whole thing, is that we
feel the Almighty would so much prefer the self-satisfied
canon to the dismal curate.   For surely the Almighty
prefers those who are self-satisfied, to those who are
always worrying.   And in any case the question must be
asked.   Did the Almighty care two pins that Jackman
should doubt His existence ?   I have already suggested
the implied conceit in the idea.   And it persists in all
those extremely pious and no doubt humble folks, who
Sunday after Sunday, think that they are paying a great
and well deserved tribute to the Deity, by singing hymns
and praying that the Unchangeable shall see fit to change.
So Miss Sinclair shows herself to be a bit of a theologian,
and it is almost amazing that a woman should know so
much of the theological worries of a curate.   I must now
examine more of Miss Sinclair's Canon Chamberlain, for
the worthy and utterly worldly Canon is a fascinating
man.

•   •   •   •   •   •   •   •   •   •   •

There is one episode in which I think that Miss Sinclair
has let her story get the better of her. The novelist
who is writing a careful study has to be very cautious that
the story does not get the bit between its teeth and turn
round and make the unfortunate novelist forsake realism,
and pander to a sudden and perhaps uncontrollable desire,
to make the tale more exciting. In a certain part of the
life of Canon Chamberlain (for Miss Sinclair's book is a
biography, even though it does not begin with birth and
does not end with death), she panders to the story and
while the episode is delightful, it is to my mind unreal
and therefore to be deplored.

Although I thoroughly distrust any generalisations
about the conduct or misconduct of the clergy, on at
least one point, it is safe to imply a general line of action.
That is, there are very few if any who would not immediately comply with the request to visit a dying person. I
do not say that they would do this necessarily from any
sense of virtue, but rather from the fact that most would
consider it to be their most important work. But quite
evidently Miss Sinclair thinks otherwise. She makes
Canon Chamberlain refuse to visit a dying woman or
rather put off the visit which is exactly the same thing.
Now I do not think that this kind of conduct is at all
likely to be found among the clergy, nor do I think that
it is really consistent with Canon Chamberlain. In
this matter I have no agreement with Miss Sinclair. I
rather think that Miss Sinclair has put the incident in to
heighten the dramatic effect. This has been achieved
but realism has suffered. And in a study of a character,
realism is of far more vital consequence than dramatic
effect. The superb state is when they can both be admirably blended. But whether the incident is realistic or

not, whether it is true or untrue, there is much delicious
atmosphere and a few quotations will show the brilliancy
of Miss Sinclair's method of treatment.

When Canon Chamberlain receives the note which
tells him to visit the dying Mrs. Tombs, he decides that
it being a very wet and unpleasing day, Mrs. Tombs must
put off her dying for twenty-four hours.   But the Canon
is obviously not *quite* easy.   And as Miss Sinclair so
admirably implies, he salves his conscience by soup !

> " At tea-time he ordered some good strong soup for
> Mrs. Tombs.   He would take it to her in the morning.
> Another reason for putting off the visit : if he went now
> there would be no soup for Mrs. Tombs ; soup to Mrs.
> Tombs was more than the consolations of religion."

This is of course admirable reasoning and up to a point
is consistent with the procrastinations of Canon Chamberlain.   Yet I still think that the Canon, soup or no soup,
would have gone *at once* to minister to Mrs. Tombs.   For
Canon Chamberlain was no fool, and to put it on the
lowest grounds, he would not have liked the diocese to
know that he had put off visiting a dying woman.   So
I think Miss Sinclair in an effort to get an exciting episode
(and it is this) has done Canon Chamberlain a distinct
injustice.   But then this may be done purposely, as it is
quite evident that she does not like the Canon much and
perhaps Miss Sinclair is too clever to like any clergy.
And no doubt the dislike is reciprocated, for though they
seldom admit it, the clergy are jealous of novelists, for
the simple reason that the clergy attract their thousands,
but the novelists attract their ten thousands.

When, in the middle of the night, Canon Chamberlain

is dragged to the bedside of Mrs. Tombs, we have a pretty accurate picture of the Canon's discomfiture in the presence of death. And perhaps the discomfort is caused by the filthy surroundings. Death is always alarming to the beholder, but it is less alarming in a luxurious bedroom, than in a stinking garret.

It is the horrid attributes of the sick room which are so appalling to Canon Chamberlain. The detestable smell of drugs is more suggestive of death than the pale glimmer of the Crucifix. Miss Sinclair describes with great discernment how odious to the fastidious Canon is the crude atmosphere of the sickening garret.

" An acrid, pungent, and sickening smell caught at his throat and choked him. The window of the room was closed and every chink in its frame was stuffed with newspaper ; an old blanket hung before it above the cotton curtains."

And it is all the hateful attributes of death that make it so difficult to see that the whole scene is really a spiritual one. It is the attempt made by those round, to keep the dying person alive, which makes the horror of the whole scene. The prayers of the priest are mixed with the odour of strong medicines, the consolations of religion are intermingled with the attempted consolations of medicine. So Miss Sinclair shows us how Canon Chamberlain is so obsessed by the physical crudity of death, that the profound spirituality of it could not pervade his senses. It is a fine piece of understanding on the part of Miss Sinclair.

" He had never got over his terror of fœtid rooms, of

the approach to the bedside. He knew that he ought to feel the pity, the solemnity, the poignancy of death ; he could feel nothing but its poison and its squalor. He couldn't rise to death's spiritual height ; every time, he came to it impotent and repugnant."

At the end of the episode, Miss Sinclair makes an unpleasant but perfectly true remark. She denotes that Canon Chamberlain was very irritated that Mrs. Tombs did not die at once, as her supposed desperate state had dragged him from his delightfully warm bed. It is a nasty thought that if people come to minister to the dying, they expect them to play fair and die, but I rather think that it is a state of affairs that exists. In many cases people who weep bitterly at the thought of someone dying, weep more bitterly when they recover, when the recovery means that the emoluments in the will are not at present theirs. In the case of the Canon, Mrs. Tombs got him out of bed, and Miss Sinclair knows that the Canon felt badly used that Mrs. Tombs in spite of his ministrations continued to live. It is a sad state of affairs for a clergyman when he recites the prayers for the dying, to find that the prayers seem to have the effect of giving a new lease of life. But the Canon retaliated by being once more a clerical snob. He allowed someone else to take poor Mrs. Tombs' funeral. This is of course correct and proper, Miss Sinclair would not make Canon Chamberlain take the funeral of a woman whose daughter was a prostitute. Thus the Canon gets his own back, Mrs. Tombs dragged him from his warm bed, she did not die in spite of his prayers for the dying but he could vent his spite on her miserable dead body.

"He made Fawcett come over from Kempston
Maisey to take Mrs. Tombs' funeral."

. . . .

It is indeed a sign of the times, when a woman novelist
can write of a Canon when he is in the genial atmosphere
of his own bed! And it is more a sign of the times when
the Canon can be written of in bed when at least half of
that bed is shared by his wife. No doubt to the *wholly*
pious, it is a little disturbing to think that so exalted a
personage as a Canon delights in the intricacies of being
in bed, it is probably more disturbing to the susceptibi-
lities of *very* pious spinsters that the said Canon should
share his nightly resting place with a wealthy and attractive widow. If we follow in the wake of Miss Sinclair,
we shall soon be allowed to read of an Archbishop in bed,
in fact there is no reason to suppose that a novel could
not be written dealing with the night life of any Archbishop. But there is no conceivable reason why the Canon
should not be written of in bed with his wife. Because
a Canon prefers not to spend his nights alone, is no reason
for supposing that the Sacraments will be outraged
thereby. Yet many people, and especially ardent
Churchwomen, imagine their clerical idols to dwell in
such a state of perpetual sanctity, that it is a little shock-
ing to them to be told that this perpetual sanctity has
its interludes of common humanity and common humanity
ensconced in a double bed!

Miss Sinclair in following the Canon to the privacy of
his double bed has written one of her most clever delicate
descriptions. I give the quotation at some length. It
is a brilliant piece of writing on a subject about which
not so much is known as ought to be!

" It was nine o'clock on a perfect morning of June.

" The Rector lay in the big double bed that had been brought from Queningford House. Downstairs, nine deep, musical strokes of the hall clock told the hour. He woke suddenly with a queer mixed sense of familiarity and strangeness. It was his own old room, but it was another bed, a bed he had not slept in before, facing the door instead of the window. He yawned and stretched himself. His arm struck gently against a warm, soft mass that he recognised as Molly, his wife. She lay there in the immense bed, with her back towards him, curled deliciously into a fat ball, her chin sunk to her breast, her knees drawn up to her waist and her heels to her hips ; like a cat, he thought affectionately, or a dormouse ; she ought to have a furry tail to cuddle her little nose in."

One more quotation from Miss Sinclair's magnificent book " A Cure of Souls " and it shall be from the very last page. There is really almost something pathetic about it, for Canon Chamberlain is deciding to give up his Orders, and whatever the cause, there is sadness about the decision.

" He saw his life stretching out before him in an unbroken succession of perfect days. Life without unpleasantness or pain. A blessed life. In a place where you could rest. A place where you could dream."

On the most important of all subjects Miss Sinclair has written her most important book. Canon Chamberlain is a sincerely drawn creation. In spite of her dislike of him Miss Sinclair has for the most part been fair to the

Canon. She has written a biographical episode of a
country rector, but it is more, it is a picture of a man who
was obviously too selfish and too worldly to be anything
but a spiritual failure. The Canon could ministrate with
soup, he could say tactful things, he could charm and win
an attractive widow but he could not bring himself to so
disregard the physical that the spiritual should be para-
mount. " A Cure of Souls " is the study of a failure, but
it is easy to condemn. It is far easier to condemn a
priest than to be one ; which is the very reason why there
are a thousand who condemn and but a few who will
risk the adventure of the priesthood.

. . . .

It must be said that in a certain sense Miss Sinclair is a
specialist. It is almost impossible to think of her as a
writer without at once being aware that she·is very much
the slave of modernism. Miss Sinclair delights in mental
states, she looks, as it were, into the minds of the characters she creates, and their speaking, is the expression of
their inmost thoughts and reasonings. She appears to
take an immense interest in what people think, she discusses problems in an easy ruminating kind of manner.
In some ways Miss Sinclair is probably the best of
present day women writers. She is infinitely superior
to the general run of women writers whose outlook is
usually in the neighbourhood of divorce, adultery and
sex hatred. Miss Sinclair, unlike most women writers,
who have not the dignity of Mrs. before their names, is
in no sense a bitter writer. She does not make all men
out as rogues and all women as saints. Rather she does
very sincerely try to be fair and no novelist can have a
more lofty and praiseworthy ideal.

Perhaps if there is one special characteristic of Miss Sinclair, it is that she is essentially an introspective writer. She seems to have an enormous understanding of life. I can imagine that Miss Sinclair knows as much about a shop girl as about an average Canon. I can imagine that she knows really accurately what shop girls think about. I think that Miss Sinclair writes with a distinct purpose and the purpose is not limited by the consideration as to how many copies will sell. She wishes to write of the minds of people, how they behave under certain circumstances, how their minds act.

Again, ill content with being merely a specialist in the delicate art of introspection, Miss Sinclair excels in the study of the uncanny. Her uncanny stories, deal again with mental states, horrid fixed ideas, those fixed ideas which being secret do not lead us to suppose that the man who chats so amiably with us, in reality is planning to batter our brains out at the first reasonable opportunity. Miss Sinclair deals with ghosts, they are not white bodiless spectres, but grim figments of a stricken conscience or an overwrought brain.

There is none of the pure and undefiled beauty in Miss Sinclair's writing which can be found in the work of Mr. Temple Thurston. Miss Sinclair is consciously clever, she is aware that what she thinks really matters, she has an idea, (it is discernible in her writings), that in some respects the Universe depends upon her. And to a certain extent it does, it is but seldom that Miss Sinclair does not make some wise and profound comment.

Miss Sinclair is, in these days of so much silliness and incompetence, intensely intellectual. It may be a reason that makes her live just out of Hampstead or just in it, I am not sure which. It might be unwise to ask whether

Miss Sinclair is a cleverer novelist than her men contemporaries. But an answer which said, that she was at least equal to them, might be a fair reply to such a question.

Miss Sinclair unlike many talented writers is equally at home with humour or pathos. She has shown, if it needed to be shown, how deep and intelligent is the mind of a brilliant woman. All her work is worth while, all is worthy of examination had I room. But I have concentrated on her splendid study of a priest but I am not forgetful of all her other fine literary achievements.

It is always an honour to a writer to be a Fellow of The Royal Society of Literature, it is perhaps a double honour when the writer thus honoured, is a novelist. And in the case of Miss Sinclair the honour is well deserved, for she is that rather rare thing, a literary novelist.

END OF PORTRAIT TWO

PORTRAIT NUMBER THREE
GILBERT FRANKAU

PORTRAIT NUMBER THREE

GILBERT FRANKAU

It is no doubt a lamentable fact, but it is nevertheless a true one, that a very large number of English people have almost completely forgotten the war. Once a year popular sentiment engages in a kind of sentimental orgy of prayer and praise and it is thought that effective communication can be made with a million dead. The press sings songs of patriotic enthusiasm, the public remains still for two minutes, at Whitehall Church dignitaries murmur a few prayers and a vast multitude having remembered the war for an hour or so disperses to as quickly as possible forget all about it.

Books that dealt with the war are now regarded as a back number, no plays that dealt with war are to be staged. But it is an excellent thing that the English should be made to remember, it is excellent that they should be reminded of the days when death was fashionable, it is excellent that they should do more than remember the Great War once a year on the 11th of November.

The war, with regard to literature resulted in a curious dualism. Those who had firmly established their literary and dramatic reputations, in writing under the influence of war, produced some of their most mediocre work. On the other hand, the war, as was only to be expected, made

the reputation of those who had yet to attain to literary
prominence. War makes poets and unmakes prose
writers, war limits the genius, war gives the impetus to
the imaginative writer who has yet to make a firm name.

Now I am perfectly aware that Mr. Frankau has produced much good work, in fact I hesitate to think that he
has produced anything that is not good. For Mr. Frankau
is a very clever man, he is so clever that he has managed
to make a large percentage of the public read what he
writes. But like most clever people, at one time, Mr.
Frankau allowed his natural cleverness to become something a little more than clever. In fact, Mr. Frankau
wandered so far from being merely clever that he became
almost a genius.

I have two perfectly straightforward reasons why I
intend to discuss " Peter Jackson " very fully in this
Essay. The first reason is that I am quite sure it is the
best book Mr. Frankau has written, the second reason
is that it is about the war. And fortunately Mr. Frankau
always writes of war as it is and not as it is pictured by
those who talk about it, to whit the armchair asses, the
episcopal prigs, the suburban women, and all the silly
public which thinks it knows more than the War Office.

The story of Peter Jackson is about something that
during the war we were so used to, that we did not realise
that we were dealing with something which was almost
Holy, something set apart that future generations might
see and might admire. This "something" was that
extraordinary concoction the civilian soldier. The civilian soldier was a curious kind of dual creature with a
soldier's body and a civilian mind. The civilian soldier
carried a rifle and had he been allowed would have wished
to carry it as the bank clerk carries a walking stick. The

civilian soldier saluted his superior officer, when had he been allowed he would have preferred to take his hat off, as though it had been a bowler. The civilian soldier, when he was shot, died in the same way as the professional soldier and in death only, was there any exact parallelism between the regular soldier and the civilian soldier. But fortunately for us, the civilian soldier learnt to become a soldier and he learnt more quickly than he had learnt to become a civilian. Mr. Frankau writes the history of a cigar merchant who became a soldier, and he writes something that is very near to the spiritual history of an ordinary man, one of those hundreds of thousands who left civil life with its civilised barbarities to become a member of the army and a sharer of its uncivilised barbarities. And let it be said that the uncivilised barbarities were not always the most difficult to bear with.

Perhaps in Peter Jackson Mr. Frankau is more a sincere artist than in any other of his work. His work is so remarkably good, that it is difficult to imagine how he could be so equally good at the very different art of popular serial writing. And serial writing, in spite of jealous highbrow critics, is a noble art, for what is written is read by the mass of intensely commonplace people who are really so important that without them there would be no world for the more distinguished to live in. If the commonplace man and woman depend for their daily bread on those who are famous and wealthy, it is equally certain that those who are famous and wealthy or famous and poor, depend for *their* fame on the commonplace masses whose sole hope in life is to get enough bread for weekdays and a little more for Sundays. And when a novelist can interest and amuse these commonplace masses, as Mr. Frankau does, then (it matters not what highly intellectual professional critics say), serial writing is a noble task. And I say this because there are those, and they are many, who say that from " Peter Jackson " to " Life and Erica " in a daily paper, is an appalling drop. I agree that there is a vast *difference* but it is intolerant and detestably selfish, to sneer at work which amuses those who toil all day and every day with no hope of fame or even moderate comfort.

It has of course to be acknowledged that certain people, who in many ways are quite human, deplore very much that the mass of people prefer serials and novels to more serious reading. It may be, that such a state of affairs is deplorable. I am not sure that the love for light fiction *is* to be deplored, at any rate there are a number of really intellectual persons, whose opinions cannot be ignored, who do regret that the mass public loves either the light novel or the serial. But we have got to construct a very different world before we arrive at conditions, when the suburban train-reading feminine public prefers Swinburne to Frankau or Chesterton to Miss Dell. And I am again not sure that the world would be vastly improved in either morality or commonsense if it fed on Swinburne and allowed " Life and Erica " to languish unread and unwept.

But it is very necessary, in any branch of literary criticism, to take the world as it is and the most talked of personality of our own day is the popular novelist. Mr. Frankau is a popular novelist because he knows perfectly well what the ordinary man and woman wants to read. Mr. Frankau is an admirable novelist for ordinary people, but he is something more, he can make extraordinary people think. And in " Peter Jackson " he performs this miracle with distinguished excellence.

One of the most dreadful things to have to listen to, is the average English civilian talking about war. When war is actually being waged, the average Englishman becomes in his own opinion a leader of an Army corps and to the astonishment of his villa or mansion family, is not called in to supersede all the professional generals. Before a war, when there are ominous rumours, when the journalists write contradictory leaders daily, when the only people who are not interested in the possibility of war are the actual soldiers, the average Englishman comes out at his best. He knows exactly how long the war will last, he knows the exact route by which the victorious British army will hack its way to an absurdly easy conquest, and while the regular troops are being quietly got to the draughty quayside, the average Englishman holds a war council and predicts the thing " won't last a week." Mr. Frankau shows us the brainlessness of the average Englishman in a delightful manner in the early stages of Peter Jackson, when there is an " idea " that war is about, when the garrulous fools who have put the State right, become war prophets who know all that the War Office never does know.

" ' If ever we do have this European war that the *Daily Mail* is so fond of talking about,' said the doctor, ' it will last about a week. Modern nerves will never stand it.' "

It might be asked how long modern nerves will stand this kind of really criminal conversation.

There might be quite a number of opinions regarding the best result that a description of lunch in The City should achieve. It might be that the description should

be perfectly accurate, so accurate that a chef could find
no fault, it might be that a lunch should be a piece of
literary staging, designed to give animation to a conversation or make an incident when events were becoming
dull. In my opinion the only proper result of the description of a lunch should be that the description should
produce actual and vulgar hunger on the part of the
reader ! When Mr. Frankau writes a description of lunch,
he means obviously that the reader shall feel hungry as
he reads and he means that the reader shall be introduced
to the spectacle of a satisfying lunch. So in Peter Jackson, Mr. Frankau writes deliciously of a lunch in The City
and it is a curious rushing affair. For you must know that
lunch in The City is a business, the chops and steaks must
be businesslike, no time here for the leisurely and playful
lunch that comes to those who sit in Piccadilly. Here
we are with Mr. Frankau in The City, and the rush and
scramble and sanctified odour are enveloping us.

"Downstairs in the Lombard, hatted men jostle at
communal tables ; steaks frizzle, crowded on the grill ;
joints appear, dwindle, disappear and are replaced ;
waiters bustle, and the girl at the cash-desk has barely
time to smile."

But though Mr. Jackson has a good deal of interest
when he is a cigar merchant in the days of peace, it is in
the days of war, that we find how splendid a novelist
Mr. Frankau is, for he is serious and Mr. Frankau, good
as he is when he is flippant, is far better when the noise of
the heavy guns is echoed from his pages.

.   .   .   .

GILBERT FRANKAU

Mr. Frankau is always serious with regard to war for the very good reason that he writes of much of it in almost a joking manner. But there is a certain anger behind the laugh and a certain contempt behind the levity. Although Mr. Frankau writes in a light way of the methods adopted when Peter Jackson applies for a commission, there is a subtle contempt for the dastardly unpreparedness for war, that was exhibited by this country, on the day when Germany was foolish enough to think that she could beat an unprepared England. She might have known that the Englishman is never so deadly as when he is unprepared. But the Kaiser was not a clever man.

That foolish monarch has now no doubt plenty of time to reflect that you cannot beat the English, because they do not know when they are beaten. But it is necessary to leave any further speculation about the Kaiser and return to Peter Jackson. The way in which he applies for his commission papers is written so convincingly by Mr. Frankau that a quotation is well worth while.

" ' This is Jackson, Sir,' began Travers. ' He was at school with me. Wants a commission. I think we ought to have him, don't you, sir ?'

" ' Done any soldiering ? ' asked Colonel Skeffington, looking up from his work.

" ' Corporal, Eton Volunteers, sir,' answered Peter.

" ' All right, Travers. Make out his Blue Paper and I'll sign it.' "

Such was the way that commissions were given to men who would be very shortly in charge of other men, when efficiency meant all the difference between life and death.

History is probably always unfair to the man or woman

who really achieves something and it is unfair because
this " something " is recorded by historians as though it
had been achieved by the famous. The curate is the
man who keeps the Church going through the centuries,
it is the curate who brings down the message of the Church
to the humble undistinguished learners, but history only
records the names of the bishops and archbishops. The
general practitioner is the man who keeps alight the lamp
of healing, it is the unknown village doctor who saves
myriads of lives, but history only records the names of the
great men of medicine. The actor and actress whose
names are always in the smallest possible print, are the
people who keep the theatre moving through the long
years, but history only records those who stand out in all
the glare that comes upon those who stand near to the
footlights.

It is not the fault of the historian, the cog must be
content to know in his own soul that without him the
wheel would be incomplete, the historian must record
those whose actions place them on the high pinnacle of
fame.

And with regard to the soldier. The soldier who is no
more than a mere unit in a countless number of platoons,
it is he who wins the war, but history is only concerned
with the high staff officers. It is not the fault of history
or the fault of the historian, it is merely the inexorable
law that those who are prominent in life will be prominent
in death, those who are obscure in life will be obscure in
death. But it is well to ponder now and then and remember that the world is kept in perpetual activity by the
obscure and it is perhaps of some consolation to those
who are obscure to be reminded of it.

But if historians must deal with giants, if historians

are forced to deal with those whose names die not, novelists can write of the plain man as much as he wishes. The novelist can construct history of the dustman, he can construct history of the shop girl, he can write the life of a prostitute, he can construct the life of a newsboy. And the mass public, which has no chance to read real history of commonplace people, can read and read with intense pleasure of imaginary people who have no claim to fame.

In " Peter Jackson " Mr. Frankau pays a crude but well deserved compliment to the ordinary soldier. The ordinary soldier must receive his laudations as one of a body but the general will receive his laudations as an individual. Mr. Frankau, almost in a Kipling manner, pays tribute to the mud-stained glorious British soldier who lived cursing and died cursing but achieved more than can ever be related in cold print.

" Let library-historians give the palm to this Field-Marshal or that Statesman if they will ; we who did our best for him know that it was the ' common man,' ' poor bloody Tommy '—on his lorry or his ration-cart, at his telephone-station or his observation post, in his trench or his gun-pit—' poor bloody Tommy,' hungry sometimes, tired mostly, frightened to the depths of his unimaginative soul, but enduring always, who staved off every British defeat and won every British victory all the way back from Mons to Compiègne and all the way forward from Compiègne back to Mons. Pray God that he find honest leaders—for without leaders and discipline he is as a child—in this future he has won for us."

When Mr. Frankau feels deeply, as he does in this passage, he rises to great heights and we are aware that he is something more than a mere teller of a story, he is in fact a very able and reasonable philosopher.

Although it is primarily the business of a novelist to write something that will entertain, it is also his business to write something that will make those who read, think.   In our own day, the preacher, spending most of his time denouncing other preachers, has deservedly lost a great deal of his influence, but the novelist, the influence of whom grows daily stronger and stronger, can be certain that what he writes will have much weight with a very large number of people who would not pay any account to the spoken words of a preacher.   One widely read novelist has more influence than the bench of bishops and had Christ made his twelve apostles to be novelists, it is impossible to say how wide His influence might have been.   Mr. Frankau always seems fully aware of the influence he has in his position as a popular novelist. Though he seldom consciously preaches, he proclaims his message by the most effective manner possible, that is by profound asides.   In this there is a marked contrast to the work of Mr. Temple Thurston.

During the military career of Peter Jackson, we get a very good insight into the kind of plotting and intrigue that persevered in the average orderly room.   While our devoted clergy were preaching the glorious crusade like parallel of the war, while our still more devoted women were running canteens and giving away white feathers, in the army itself officers were taking part in many low schemes to further promotion.   By means of dialogue Mr. Frankau gives an instance of this inside plotting which is well worth recording at some length.

The plot concerns an adjutant and the environment is
" somewhere in England " and the melancholy fact is
that it might be anywhere.

" Peter deliberately took off his cap, and sat down
at the Colonel's table.

" ' Can't we pull together, P.J. ?' went on Locksley.
' You know I can do you much more good than your
pal Bromley. There's your second star, for instance.'

Peter couldn't help admiring the audacity of the
fellow. He wanted to consolidate his position ; didn't
care how, so long as he achieved his purpose.

" ' And supposing I were to tell the C.O. what you've
just suggested ?'

" ' He wouldn't believe you—any more than he
believed Bareton. The old man's as weak as water.
You know that as well as I do.'

" Peter controlled the impulse to hit Locksley in the
face, and asked : ' Is that all ?'

" ' Oh, of course,' Locksley fell into the trap, ' when we
come to allotting the captaincies. . . . Let's see '—
he referred to a list—' you haven't got any captains
in ' B ' yet. If the Major goes—'

" This was news indeed. Now Peter saw the plan
whole. With complacent Company Commanders and
a weak Colonel, Locksley's position would be unique.

" ' Is the Major going ?' he asked, playing for time.

" ' Between you and me and the gatepost,' Locksley
winked, ' the W.O. has just asked if he is " considered
fit to command a battalion ".' "

And then Mr. Frankau adds a rather poignant footnote.

" Meanwhile men died in Flanders."

And it might well be added, while men died in Flanders, wallowed in mud in Flanders, resorted with French prostitutes in Flanders, drank Café at the Estaminets in Flanders, thought, dreamed of, consumed in irrational quantities bully beef in Flanders, men in England used all their brains to swindle those who were in Flanders, women in England used all their brains to " work " promotion, the press in England complained bitterly of the awful fact that aeroplanes had bombed civilians.

" MEANWHILE, MEN DIED IN FLANDERS."

.   .   .   .

Humanity is always liable to forget that the hardest part of war is not necessarily that which is undergone in actual battle.   The man who effects a wonderful act of heroism under fire, deserves the Victoria Cross, but the man who marched twenty-five kilometres along the pavé roads when his feet swam in their own blood, deserves the Victoria Cross even more.   The way to Calvary was no doubt a long way, the road to Tipperary longer, but the pavé road to the trenches was the longest of all.

Perhaps no horror of all the horrors that the war provided was so horrible as the march, when men would give their souls to fall out and would have sold their birthrights twice over for a mess of pottage.   Mr. Frankau has caught the horror of the march against hunger with a grim realism.

" Peter stepped back ; and the Company plodded by. As they passed him, sweating heads turned, dusty lips murmured: 'Can't you do nuffink for us, sir ?   Just a bite, sir. Anyfink 'll do, sir.' They looked like faithful dogs whose masters had betrayed them.

" ' Cheer up, lads,' said Peter, ' Cheer up !'

" ' We'll do our best, sir. Bit 'ard, though, our first time in action, ain't it, sir ? . . .'

" The files trudged past him in the dust. Behind them came other files, thousands of them. All dust stained. All sleepless. All hungry. ' Food ' they cried as the marched. ' Food.' "

And those who forget the war, those who made gain out of the stinking corpses of men, those who have forgotten " poor bloody Tommy," let them mark, read and if they can, learn.

" But not a man of them fell out !"

.   .   .   .

I suppose one of the strangest attributes of war is the psychology of fear. Fear is the one definite thing no soldier must *show*. The greater the danger, the greater the torrent of high explosive shells, the greater the imminent danger of a sudden and violent death, the more it is expected that the soldier will preserve a *sang froid* that he would adopt in walking down some quiet suburban street to his own humble and sedate home.

The private soldier, deafened by the continuous thunder and whistle of giant shell cracks, must be calm and even dignified. The officer nearly driven mad by the incessant whine of hungry bullets, eager for their prey, must retain a dignity of bearing and even insist on being saluted. The general mapping out a great action, treating a battalion as an army of machine-like pawns, must show no emotion,

he must quietly carry on, while an aerial bomb kills the
sentry outside G.H.Q. and disembowels a staff captain.

And, surprising as it may be to those who have not
been " under fire," most soldiers do not show fear, if
they feel it, and young soldiers for the first time under
shell fire present a curious psychology which is remarked
upon with considerable skill by Mr. Frankau.

" Men under fire for the first time are not usually
frightened."

This is perfectly true, men under shell fire for the first
time are merely curious.

.   .   .   .

Possibly one of the most outstanding characteristics
of Mr. Frankau is his extraordinary ability for making a
true remark about some method of conduct.   Quite a
number of people are only noteworthy in so far as what
they say is almost invariably untrue.   The reverse is
the case with Mr. Frankau.   Not content with being a
mere novelist, Mr. Frankau is also a philosopher and he is
such an admirable philosopher that I very much doubt
if legitimate philosophers and philosophies know much
about him !

Mr. Frankau in " Peter Jackson " has a very sane
remark to make about public school boys.   He gets the
essential reason why those who are not of the public
school persuasion dislike those who are.   The public
school boy is a type, he is as different from the grammar
school boy, as the lady is from the suburban woman who
dresses like a lady.   It is almost impossible to define the

difference. In regard to the army ; the public school boy calls the artillery the " gunners," the grammar school boy calls them the artillery. The lady calls the engineers the " sappers," the suburban woman calls them the engineers. And between these modes of speech lie all the differences that make class. I will quote what Mr. Frankau says about the dislike of the public school boy. It is so deliciously true and if you like to say that it is all hatefully snobbish, you can say and say it until you are tired of saying it, for class distinction has always been and always will be. Try as much as you will, those who call the artillery the " gunners " will not readily mix with those who call the artillery, the artillery. And those who call the engineers, the engineers, will always (be they of either sex) think those who call them, " the sappers," arrant and disgusting snobs. And the fact that they will be probably painfully right, won't alter the state of affairs.

" The Weasel who happened to have been at Winchester before going on to Woolwich, felt suddenly and immensely superior to everybody on earth. For, on that point, all old English public school men feel alike ; which is what makes them at times so insufferable to outsiders. If an outsider had asked any of the men in that cellar why he was fighting, the outsider would have met with an incredulous lift of the eyebrow ; that particular lift of the eyebrow which no outsider understands ; but which conveys—to one who can interpret—' My dear fellow, I was at Eton, (or Winchester, or Haileybury, or Harrow, or Radley, or a hundred other of those foundations which pacific intellectuals, affect to despise) and one does, don't you know, one just does.'

" Luckily there is no education at English public schools. They merely train boys to be men."

Mr. Frankau wisely does not say, that in this high ambition, the public schools do not always succeed.

.　　.　　.　　.　　.　　.　　.　　.　　.　　.　　.

On a very great subject, Mr. Frankau has written a really great novel and the probable reason that this novel is great, is that Mr. Frankau quite certainly set out to write a sincere picture of a civilian soldier. That he has succeeded in this is perfectly apparent to anyone who reads " Peter Jackson."

It might seem almost impertinence to attempt to say what Mr. Frankau's position is in literature, or if you will insist on a distinction, fiction in our own time. We live in an extremely critical age, the man who can become a " best seller " has some remarkable power about him. Mr. Frankau is deservedly one of the most widely read novelists of the present day. His books are full of his delightful and genial personality. There is no pessimism about them. The people who live, and they do actually live, in Mr. Frankau's books, are those lovable and exasperating people, amongst whom, " we live and move and have our being."

Mr. Frankau is an extraordinary student of human nature, he knows exactly how certain people act under certain circumstances. He can write of the hoarse and cheery laughter of joyful humanity, he can write of the sob and tears of humanity oppressed by melancholy. There is a very remarkable sanity about Mr. Frankau and unlike many successful authors, he does not seek publicity by means of a retiring modesty. The public which reads books in lifts, in tube trains, in rattling

omnibuses, this is much of the public that adores Mr.
Frankau. And the homage is well deserved, sympathy
stands out pre-eminent in Mr. Frankau's work.

Mr. Frankau is the novelist for the average man and
the average woman and the novelist who can interest
this heterogenous mass is not very far short of the state
of being a genius. And it is quite likely that he is something more than a genius. It may be urged and urged
with truth that some of Mr. Frankau's work is coarse.
And it is an excellent merit that this should be so. Not
that coarseness is a merit, but that humanity is naturally
coarse, and the novelist who would write of humanity
must of necessity be coarse at times.

The novelist cannot write truly of a civilian soldier
and let him refrain from designating much of his surroundings as " bloody " squared. You cannot write of a
prostitute and expect her to think that fornication is a
deadly sin. You cannot write of a bishop and expect
him to publicly be in favour of free love. The novelist
must write of people as they are. And it is the most
essential characteristic of Mr. Frankau that he is such
a sincere artist that he makes coarse people, coarse,
vulgar people, vulgar, refined people, refined.

And there is a vast difference in being coarse for the
sake of realism and in being coarse just for its own sake.
People love above all to read of themselves, that is why
they read what Mr. Frankau writes. People love to
see themselves in a book, that is why they like to read
what Mr. Frankau says of them. Humanity is ever
curious and wishful to regard itself in a mirror. Mr.
Frankau makes his books like a number of mirrors, the
average man or woman, see themselves reflected in them,
and they see themselves reflected truly.

Mr. Frankau laughs with humanity, but he does not laugh at it. He knows what life is in the stalls, but he has also sat in the gallery. Mr. Frankau is a very human writer, but he has ideas of God. Mr. Frankau writes a love story because a love story is life.

Mr. Frankau is still a young man but he has already a world wide reputation as a novelist. He has by dint of sincere and masterly writing placed himself in the front rank of living novelists. Certain superior people may be inclined to regard Mr. Frankau with an amused tolerance, but it is well to remember that superior people are not immune from jealousy. The public trusts Mr. Frankau and when it wants to be entertained it turns to him. And Mr. Frankau being thoroughly aware of this " turning," does more than merely entertain, he instructs.

It is a healthy sign that a novelist of the sincerity of Mr. Frankau can find such a response among the masses of the people. For no matter whether sincerity be desperately vulgar or puritanically modest, a love for sincerity and truth is an admirable sign. Whether you think Mr. Frankau coarse or whether you think him delicate does not matter. The public loves the books of Mr. Frankau, not because they *may* be coarse or because they *may* be delicate, they love them because they *are* true and a sincere picture of life as it is lived by men and women.

END OF PORTRAIT THREE

PORTRAIT NUMBER FOUR
HUGH WALPOLE

PORTRAIT NUMBER FOUR

HUGH WALPOLE

THERE are few novelists, who peer down at the fundamentals, with so close a scrutiny as Mr. Walpole. With an air of almost exultant joy he lays bare the very soul of men. His books, are terrible books, because they are true. The most terrible of all truths is truth. The terror of life is most apparent when nothing very remarkable is happening.

Let a nation be devastated by gigantic war, let it be almost decimated by an earthquake, let a city be uprooted by a callous hurricane and people, in their terror and dismay enunciate that God is a brute. But let a nation pursue its even tenour, let no outstanding event shake its lethargic inhabitants into unwilling thought and all is thought to be well and God is no longer a brute, in fact few give Him even a passing thought. Yet while the nation is pursuing its even way, men and women are choked by the deadly grip of cancer, lust fills the hospitals, lunatic asylums and prisons, the Churches quarrel over candles and apostolic succession and chant in a half hearted way a melancholy Hallelujah.

Mr. Walpole deals with the naked cruelty and toil of ordinary life. He sees life ever a hard experience, playing with those who pass along its alleys, as though they were

77

mere helpless, humble pawns, driven here, driven there, so fast, so inevitably that none can say whence they come or whither they go. It is perhaps a melancholy picture, but it is the more melancholy in that it is so terribly true.

In the opinion of the writer, the book that is most characteristic of Mr. Walpole, when he is in a mood of passionate sincerity is most certainly " Fortitude." And the book that shows Mr. Walpole in his other mood, that of a mystic, is most shown in " The Golden Scarecrow." While admitting that all Mr. Walpole's work is worthy of attention, as my space is limited, I shall con fine myself to an examination of " Fortitude " and " The Golden Scarecrow."

.   .   .   .

"Fortitude " is, in the best sense, a brilliant analytical study. Intensity of passion is intermingled with great powers of restraint. One of the marked characteristics of Mr. Walpole is his sense of proportion, he does not allow deep feelings to destroy his natural dignity and superb self-control. Mr. Walpole employs the most effective method of attack, he writes with a deadly cold-ness, such a method of onslaught is far preferable to violent denunciation. That is why, apart from his unassailable position, a judge, when he condemns in cold tones, is so much more deadly than the blaspheming, illogical, senseless, street corner and public park orator. Coldness is a far more deadly weapon than insensate heat. The cold writer, able to rely on his judgment, is far more formidable than the impulsive writer, who breaks into violent dialectic and forgets that logic is a useful force.

" Fortitude " is a model of a coldly carefully written book. It could so easily have led its writer into excesses of anger, it could so easily have led to wild and sensational statements. With the acumen of the true novelist, who is also an artist, Mr. Walpole has kept his rather dreadful picture under a rigid control. At the same time, when necessary, we are not spared, realism is unpleasant, Mr. Walpole does not shirk his duty.

It has been my fate to read many descriptions of thrashings, thrashings at school, thrashings while the sea eats at the ship, thrashings of brutes, thrashings by brutes. But I do not remember having read a more admirable description of a thrashing than that written by Mr. Walpole in " Fortitude." This description is almost painful to read, the cold fury of the father is a horrible reality. The tenacious and obstinate courage of his unfortunate son is so terrific that we almost feel the father is thrashing a machine. The terrible hatred that there is between father and son is a tremendous reminder that the most deep-rooted loathing is often to be found between those who are most intimately connected. The affection of blood relations is an inscrutable Divine mystery, but the hatred of blood relations is an unfathomable Devilish mystery because it destroys all our ideas of what ought to be. Mankind expects enemies to hate each other, mankind does not expect father and son to engage in this pitiful emotion. And when mankind meets such a contingency, it is baffled, it is shocked, it is inclined to chafe at those who demand that the Universe is a rational entity.

While the whole of Mr. Walpole's picture of this thrashing is dramatic, it is never melodramatic. While it grips the reader as in a vice, there is a conscious feeling that all

Mr. Walpole cares for, is that his scene shall be enacted
with scrupulous care and deep sincerity. The piece of
writing is Mr. Walpole at his very best. It is the very
acme of savagery, not the pure savagery of the heathen
barbarian, but the impure savagery of the civilised barbarian.

The detestable scene is enacted on Christmas Eve and
Mr. Walpole is not *making* drama by putting the thrashing at Christmas time. Christmas, though it is the time
when most men and women turn to thoughts of charity,
is also the time when the most savage events take place.
I shall give the whole melancholy scene at some length.

" ' You must learn obedience. Take off your night-
shirt.'

" He took it off, and was a very small naked figure in
the starlight, but his head was up now and he faced his
father.

" ' Bend over the bed.'

" He bent over the bed, and the air from the window
cut his naked back. He buried his head in the counter-
pane and fastened his teeth in it so that he should not
cry out.

" During the first three cuts he did not stir, then an
intolerable pain seemed to move through his body—
it was as though a knife were cutting his body in half.
But it was more than that—there was terror with him
now in the room ; he heard that little singing noise
that came through his father's lips, he knew that his
father was smiling."

Perhaps the last line is the key to the whole situation.
There is nothing so dreadful as cruelty accompanied by a

smile. We may not like the executioner who carries
out his work with an expression of angry contempt, but
we should hate the executioner who smiled as the prisoner
was hanged. Mr. Walpole wishes us to know that the
father *enjoyed* thrashing his son, it was a physical lust
and the blows satiated the lust. Therefore the father
smiled. It is the perfection of word painting.

If the description of the beating is terrible, the reaction
when it is over is no less appalling. It is perhaps even
more appalling than the beating. For while the beating
is in progress there is the hope that it will end soon. But
when it is all over, there is only the eternal misery to
contemplate stretching away and away and across the
horizon and on for ever and ever.

There is such a penetrating analogy to the desperate
fight that is waged in the sick room. The amazing
optimism of man is such that even though the patient
be within a few minutes of dissolution, we fight on and on
and hope that the angel of death may yet be made to
wait longer for his prey. It is only when the jaw has
dropped, when the face has become firmly set, when the
eyes are wide open and see not, when the priest has
finished his prayer, when the doctor has left the room, it
is then that we scream madly or sob bitterly, for the time
being, all is over and there is no future.

Mr. Walpole with amazing skill gives us the picture
of the beaten boy, unbeaten by the slash of the blows, but
beaten by the dread prospect of a future of unending
misery.

The father has finished his beating of his son and this
is the bitter climax.

" The door closed. Very slowly he raised himself,

but moving was torture ; he put on his night shirt
and then quickly caught back a scream as it touched
his back.   He moved to the window and closed it,
then he climbed very slowly on to his bed and the
tears that he had held back came, slowly at first, and
then more rapidly, at last in torrents.   It was not the
pain, although that was bad, but it was the misery
and the desolation and the great heaviness of a world
that held no hope, no comfort, but only a great cloud
of unrelieved happiness.

" At last, sick with crying, he fell asleep."

It must be recollected that in writing " Fortitude "
Mr. Walpole is writing something more than a mere
novel, he is writing a dissertation on courage and the
dauntless determination of Peter Westcott to attain to
that most excellent, but elusive virtue.

It is therefore only to be expected that Mr. Walpole
will present to us something that is like a series of episodes
with a picture of Westcott as the principal character in
each of them.   Such a method is probably the most
admirable for a penetrating character study.   The story,
though it is there, is in importance but a secondary
matter.   Yet the skill of Mr. Walpole is so illuminating
that in " Fortitude " we have quite a good story.   But
the importance of the book, in my opinion, is the study of
Westcott and his fierce fight to retain his courage at all
times and in all situations.   And Mr. Walpole enacts the
strange irony of life with truth and perception.   The
man who determines to have courage is placed in many
situations in which he can demonstrate his affection for
the virtue.   The man who cares not about courage, who
gets along easily, who cries out rather than not cry out

when he is hurt, more often than not is not placed in situations which demand much use of courage. Mr. Walpole, intent on a study of courage, gives us in Peter Westcott just the type of person who is likely to find himself in positions where much courage is needed. Mr. Walpole is a most careful artist, his characters and situations seem to me to blend admirably.

Not very long after Peter has had his thrashing and met the infliction with Stoical courage, Mr. Walpole gets Peter to school. And Peter is just the type of boy who will get a bad time there. No one is so hated at a school, with the exception of the headmaster, as the obstinate boy, the boy who will not be beaten, the boy who is not afraid of the prefects, the boy upon whom the thrusting bully makes little or no impression. There is a splendid scene when the whole school hisses Peter Westcott, yet Westcott, is immovable. Westcott reports a boy who gets whisky to make a small boy drunk and the boy who is reported is none other than a great cricketer.

The great cricketer is expelled and the mass of schoolboys who would forgive Satan if he were a good bat, boycott Westcott and make him very nearly lose his self control, but, delightful realist is Mr. Walpole, not quite. The boy, standing alone beats the frenzied and hissing mob, just as the curious figure on the Calvary Cross has always beaten the sneering intellectuals, the pious priests and the blaspheming enemies, who have smashed the Cross into a thousand pieces only to find it still there, lonely and unafraid.

" They made way in silence as he passed quietly to the other end of the gymnasium and stood, a little above them, on the steps that led to the gallery. He started

the roll-call with the head of the school and the sixth
form . . . . there was no answer to any name ; only
perfect silence and every eye fixed upon him. For a
wild moment he wished to burst out upon them, to
crash their heads together, to hurt—then his self-
control returned. Very quietly and clearly he read
through the school list, a faint smile on his lips. Bobby
Galleon was the only boy, out of the three hundred, who
answered."

And Westcott is not beaten, he is much more, not
beaten, than when his father thrashed him. Mr. Walpole
is delineating his evolution with great care.

" ' Well,' said Peter, throwing a clod of dark, scented
earth into the air and losing sight of it in the black
about him—' Here's to next year's battle !' "

If we wish to criticise Mr. Walpole from what may
perhaps be called a " Literary " standpoint, it may be
well to say something about his power of dialogue. Mr.
Walpole quite evidently writes his dialogue with the most
scrupulous care. We can almost see as we read, the heavy
mental battle which Mr. Walpole experiences, as his
dialogue emerges from his mind and advances to the
printed page. All the psychology that is so necessary to
successful dialogue is there. The question asked is
answered by the reply that we should expect. The
mental attitude of the speakers and their mental effects
on each other, are brought out, by Mr. Walpole, with truly
astonishing skill.

I think that this remarkable use of dialogue by Mr.
Walpole is well illustrated in an extraordinary passage

HUGH WALPOLE

in which Westcott accuses his father of killing his mother. And the " killing " is a much more terrible process, than a mere straightforward murder, for it is something that has been proceeding subtly by inches and there is no punishment except conscience. And Westcott's father is not bothered very greatly by his conscience !

The whole passage of words between Westcott and his detestable brute of a father is a model of dignity and restraint, yet there is a deep sense of drama pervading the whole scene. Just before his mother dies, Westcott by a significant sentence alters the relationship between himself and his father. For the future Westcott will openly show his hatred, it will no longer be a secret feeling.

> " ' You have been with your mother ? '"
> " ' Yes.'
> " ' You have done her much harm. She is dying.'
> " ' I know everything,' Peter answered, looking him in the face."

Then when the soul of the ill-used woman has escaped the cruelty of man, when the shadow of death has enveloped the house, when the father and son face each other, Peter storms out his awful accusation, and it is the more awful in that it is so undeniably true. It is a splendid piece of human understanding on the part of Mr. Walpole.

> " In the darkened dining-room, later, his father stood in the doorway, with a candle in his hand, and above it his white face and short black hair, shone as though carved from marble.
> " Peter came from the window towards him. His father said : ' You killed her by going to her.'

" Peter answered :
" ' All these years you have been killing her.' "

Such a passage as this demonstrates beyond all shadow
of doubt, the tremendous understanding that Mr. Walpole
has of the significance of dialogue.   It has been said that
a certain eminent novelist, whose name appears in the press
with almost the frequency of an eminent politician, has
said that two lines of dialogue take him an hour to write.
It may be suggested that this rate of work may seem too
rapid for Mr. Walpole.

.   .   .   .

After so much tragedy it is refreshing to find Mr.
Walpole something of a student, of no less a district than
Bloomsbury, that delightful part of London, which is not
the West End, but is the introduction to the West End,
and is the first stopping place for provincials who come
to see the " sights " of London, those sights the Londoner
seldom sees, because he sees them every day.
    But Mr. Walpole is almost libellous about Bloomsbury,
he quite evidently knows nothing about it.   In fact he
writes something that he hardly ever does write, that is
pure and unadulterated nonsense.   Listen to Mr. Walpole, you who love the dirty brown and grey of Bloomsbury.

" Bloomsbury is Life on Thirty Shillings a week without the drama of starvation or the tragedy of the
embankment, but with all the ignominy of making
ends meet under the stern and relentless eye of a
boarding house keeper."

Mr. Walpole is quite wrong. All he says refers to that desert of pseudo respectability which lies on the wrong side of the Park. I mean Bayswater. Bayswater with its army of pathetic spinsters, Bayswater with its Greek Church and its numerous other Churches, Bayswater with its hopeful widows, its charred Anglo-Indians, its nondescript population which lives and dies in boarding houses, it is in Bayswater that life in a boarding house is " ignominy."

Bloomsbury is an intellectual city which dwells under the shadow of the British Museum, Bayswater is a residential collection of weird humanity, which comes from all the ends of the earth and exists until, one by one, it passes to the earth, mourned by the boarding-house keeper who has lost several pounds a week, through the behaviour of the principal actor in the undertakers procession.

Bloomsbury is just near to the pleasure land of London, Bayswater is just away from the end of it. The difference is amazing. Mr. Walpole in " Fortitude " writes rubbish about Bloomsbury, it is a cruel libel, for Bloomsbury is too artistic, too good-natured, to allow starvation on thirty shillings a week For such a sum it gives no food, so those who cannot pay more do not *live* in Bloomsbury, and I doubt if they even live in Bayswater.

All through the book, after Peter has left home and sailed forth into the world, Mr. Walpole lets us know and know only too well, that Peter's life is one series of disappointments. It is not exactly a tragedy, but very, very nearly so. Peter writes books and the world is unmoved. Peter has a son, his son was to do all that which his father had hoped to do, the little fellow dies and millions of others continue to live.

Peter's wife never quite understands Peter and Peter never quite understands his wife. It is with regard to the marriage failure of Peter that I think Mr. Walpole makes an aside, which is possibly one of the essential reasons for the non-success of many marriages. I do not mean those marriages which end in the divorce, I mean those marriages which are one long unending bickering and dissatisfaction to all parties.

" He had expected Clare to be like himself, had made no allowance for differences of temperament."

It is one of the most essential reasons for marriage failure. Two people cannot be alike. It is ridiculous to think that the marriage rite necessarily makes two people think the same, feel the same about life, look out upon events through the same perspective.

If people would remember differences of temperament, there would be less fatuous talk about the merging of individuality by marriage and the consequent misery and failure.

It is extremely interesting to find Mr. Walpole writing of the subtle and inevitable way in which Westcott's book did not attract the attention he expected.   No book can do what its author expects it to do, for every author thinks that the world will notice his book, whereas he has to be " content " that the world has condescended to publish his book at all.   The description of the failure of Peter's novel is so admirably done by Mr. Walpole that a quotation is not out of place.   It is one more spoke in the wheel, nothing goes really right for Westcott, he has always to call up his hidden stores of courage.

" But Peter was now in a fever that saw an enemy round every corner. The *English News Supplement* only gave him a line :—*Mortimer Stant*. A new novel by the author of Reuben Hallard, depicting agreeably enough the amorous adventures of a stockbroker of middle age."

There is the inevitable and depressing climax of which Mr. Walpole writes sympathetically.

" For six weeks the book lingered in the advertisements. A second edition, composed for the most part of an edition for America, was announced, there was a belated review or two . . . . and then the end."

The whole episode is so intensely human, Mr. Walpole is dealing with life and life in his skilful hands is made into a fine story.

. . . .

" Fortitude " is a book of overwhelming reality. It teems with life, life lived in an attitude of hardness that is akin to granite. The whole atmosphere is sombre, gloomy, but it is not hopeless. Westcott never loses his courage, never gives in. Blows, though they are severe ones, ricochet off him, as a bullet ricochets off a hard substance.

Mr. Walpole, as I have said, writes his fine study with a passionate sincerity. We are face to face with life and life in Mr. Walpole's book is a harsh experience. Westcott is so determined to be courageous that he is almost unpleasant. The very determined person, virtuous as

he may be, is not the most delightful of companions.
Though it may be a detestable vice, a certain amount of
weakness, of giving in, makes a man quite often a genial
good natured soul. The prostitute is a pleasanter person
to encounter than the rescue worker, the one has lost her
courage and has given in, the other has kept her courage
and has not been beaten. And the beaten person is a
pleasanter person, more often than not, to deal with.
Westcott is terrifically stubborn, his perpetual determination to keep his courage, makes him obstinate and
liable to look for offence where none is intended.

Mr. Walpole has carved out Westcott's character with
the most scrupulous care and discrimination. He is on
his side, at the same time he shows us how in some ways
Peter is his own enemy. Mr. Walpole is not afraid to
show the weakness of someone for whom, for the most
part, he has a profound admiration.

There is a magnificent ending to this epic of courage,
a glorious ending, an ending that the whole book has led
us gently towards. Mr. Walpole ends his book, almost as
though it were a passage from The Revelation of Saint
John, that glorious vision real or unreal as you will, which
is never read without giving the reader a faint idea of the
impenetrable glory of the things that come after.

" He answered the storm—
" ' Make of me a man—to be afraid of nothing—to
be ready for everything—Love, friendship, success . . .
to take if it comes . . . to care nothing if these things
are not for me. . .'
" ' Make me brave. Make me brave !'
" He fancied that once more against the wall of the
sea mist he saw, tremendous, victorious, the Rider on

the Lion. But now, for the first time, the Rider's
face was turned towards him.

" And Behold—he was the Rider !"

.   .   .   .

" The Golden Scarecrow " is something that requires
the most gentle treatment possible, but this is not to say
that, therefore, it merits no criticism. A thing of pure
beauty, though it may appeal to all the senses, may have
to undergo criticism on the grounds as to whether it is
utilitarian. Criticism depends entirely on point of view.
We may criticise the Catholic Church adversely, not
because we dislike the miracle of bread and wine becoming
blood and water but because we object to the ambition of
Italy to be a supernatural nation and leader of the world
that embraces Christendom. Such a criticism is fair
if it is always recognised that the hostility to Catholism in
my example is on the grounds of its political wishes. I
merely cite the Catholic Church as an instance. Let me
proceed to the other extreme. On the ground that
Rationalism attempts to make everything only true, by
experience, we may support that movement. On the
other hand, we may roundly condemn Rationalism because
it destroys, or attempts to destroy, the doctrinal dogmas of
the Orthodox Churches. In a word criticism largely
depends on point of view and our *a priori* positions.

Let us apply this proposition to the question of " The
Golden Scarecrow."

Now say what you will, no one will surely deny that the
whole idea of " The Golden Scarecrow " is a beautiful
impossibility. But because it is a beautiful impossibility
is no reason whatever for denying that it may have

practical use.   And I assume that Mr. Walpole meant his book to be something more than a beautiful impossibility, I assume he meant it to stand for something definite.

Now whatever you like to say about Christ, whether you make Him the Supreme Ruler of The Universe, or the absolute messenger of God, or a mere splendid teacher or if you go to the other extreme, and call Him a dangerous lunatic, He cannot be ignored.   I say whatever you feel about this astounding Person, no one the world has ever yet seen has had so much publicity.

In " The Golden Scarecrow " Mr. Walpole talks about a shadowy being who appears every now and then to certain little children.   And each of these children looks upon this shadowy being as a Friend.   At first sight most people will say this is both a beautiful and a useful conception. They will say, that there is no better way of starting a child's religion than by telling him of a Friend, who is something Supernatural.   But Mr. Walpole makes his children in " The Golden Scarecrow " become aware of this Friend, they quite naturally talk to Him.

As I have said this is very beautiful, and it is so beautiful that one is tempted to leave the whole matter and not probe too deeply.   At the same time, if a man constructs a kind of child's religion, he cannot expect to have no criticism of it.

My objection to the Friend idea in " The Golden Scarecrow " is not based on any objection to such a possible Being.   My objection is based on the fact that I think it is untrue to say that children have any conception of a Supernatural Being, unless they are distinctly told.   I mean this.   The average mother tells the average child that God is a kindly being who will be cross if little boys tell lies or steal jam, or will be pleased if little boys do not

lie or do not steal jam. And the little boys (or little girls)
believe this, not because they believe in any God idea, but
because they firmly believe that their mother's do not say
that which is not true. Or take it this way. Suppose a
mother told her little boy that the Being he had to pray
to was a Being with fifty heads and seventy tails, I say
that the little boys would believe just as readily as though
he were told of " The Friend for little Children " who
dwells " above the deep blue sky."

Is it useful then to suggest, as Mr. Walpole does most
strongly suggest, that children are aware of a kind of
shadowy Friend, who talks with them and talks over their
childish fears and hopes and joys ? If we are content to
take it as mere *idea* that makes a beautiful book, there
can be no conceivable harm in the suggestion. But if we
take the idea in " The Golden Scarecrow " as a true picture of a child's mind, then I think that the whole theory
is open to grave objections. I do not think that children
have an innate idea of Christ, I do not think that they have
any conception of such a Person until they are told of
Him by adults.

I do not think that the child's religion is anything more
than that which he is told by his elders. If it be argued
that children may see visions, that we who are so detestably grown up cannot see, then why is it that children,
as a rule, are silent on such a matter ? Children are the
very last people to keep things to themselves and I have
never personally met any child, who talked about any
such vision as the vision accorded to the children in Mr.
Walpole's book. Again I say I only criticise " The Golden
Scarecrow " on the grounds of truth. On the grounds of
romantic beauty I have no quarrel with Mr. Walpole's
philosophy of the child's religion whatever. But I do

think that fundamentally the child's religion is a dependent thing, that it is derived and is not spontaneous.

Of course there is just the possibility that the teaching of " The Golden Scarecrow " is even dangerous. Those (and they are many and are deeply serious thinkers) who object to the idea of a Personal God, may well consider that the suggestion of a material or spiritual Friend who can appear, is mischievous.

I do not in the least agree with them, I merely state their position. I consider most strongly that every child should be taught the conception of a Personal God, I do not care whether the conceptional is either unscientific or unphilosophical. The adult mind may grasp what is meant by an Impersonal Force or an Absolute or a Categorical Imperative, but the child must, at first, be taught by a process of anthropomorphism, when it comes to reason, it can make its own conception.

To sum up. I object to " The Golden Scarecrow " merely on the grounds that I think Mr. Walpole does not know the child's mind, at the same time, his romantic idea is so beautiful that his possibly irrational thought can be forgiven.

.   .   .   .

In some ways Mr. Walpole is probably the most serious novelist of the present day. It may not be an exaggeration to say that his work is of the very highest quality. There is never the very slightest suggestion of any vulgarity in his work. Mr. Walpole writes of life as it is, he does not *make* a story, the story makes itself. It proceeds naturally and logically to its appointed end. I have spent my time on " Fortitude " and " The Golden Scarecrow " because out of much splendid work I have thought

that these two books show two very different sides of Mr.
Walpole's outlook.

It has been said that as a rule, a distinguished father
does not have a distinguished son. In the case of Mr.
Walpole the contradictory is true. A distinguished father
(a bishop of the Scottish Episcopal Church) has in Mr.
Walpole a far more distinguished son. To-day the bishops
" slay their thousands," but the novelists " slay their
ten thousands."

A novelist born in the bosom of the dignified sanctity
of the Church, Mr. Walpole has become a novelist for the
people. And he is this because he is a simple sympathetic
student in spite of his vast and amazing intellect.

END OF PORTRAIT FOUR

PORTRAIT NUMBER FIVE

W. B. MAXWELL

PORTRAIT NUMBER FIVE

W. B. MAXWELL

I CANNOT think of any living novelist who is a more *pleasant* writer than Mr. Maxwell. At the same time this pleasantness does not make him, in any way, shirk unpleasant situations. Even the most unpleasant episode is approached by Mr. Maxwell in a pleasant manner. This is probably caused by Mr. Maxwell's evident genial outlook upon life.

It would I think be impossible to find any other novelist of to-day who is so clever at describing the trivialities of life as Mr. Maxwell. In the various extracts which I shall examine, taken from his work, I shall endeavour to consider various aspects of Mr. Maxwell which make up his brilliant and unfailingly attractive equipment.

·   ·   ·   ·   ·   ·   ·

The world can show no more delightful spectacle than the sincere friendship of two people of the same sex. The friendship of two men is probably on a higher level than the friendship of two women, because I believe sincerely that men are less likely to be jealous than women.

In " The Day's Journey " Mr. Maxwell writes an extraordinary illuminating study of two men friends. I am not going to say that this is Mr. Maxwell's best book, but

it is a very good book and like many good books it is not
as well known as it ought to be.   It is certainly not as well
known as some of Mr. Maxwell's other books.   I think
for the reason that it is a different type of book.   It is
much more a study and much less a romance.   And it is a
book that richly deserves a certain amount of attention.

Mr. Maxwell seems to have an almost uncanny grip of
character, he not only knows intimately what a man says,
he knows what a man *thinks*.   And a person who has
this power is a very dangerous person to meet!   Yet
Mr. Maxwell is one of the most lovable personalities that
fiction has produced for a very long time.   And his books
are equally lovable.

A certain cynic remarking on what was required to
make a novel successful said that there must be a touch of
vulgarity about it.   Mr. Maxwell has confounded that
cynic utterly.   You may find many things in the work of
Mr. Maxwell, you will find love, hate, domesticity, dis-
content, madness, laughter, tears, but try as you will,
you will not find anything which can be called vulgarity.
Even if you give the widest application to the word, so
that it extends from over jewelled women to under clothed
vampires or from over dressed cads to under dressed
tramps, you will not find the state of vulgarity in Mr.
Maxwell's books.   And, miraculous as it may be, Mr.
Maxwell is enormously popular.   Look over the shoulder
of the girl sitting next to you in the tube.   She is reading
Maxwell.   Look through the chink in the curtain, gaze
into the little suburban room, watch the man or woman
quietly reading near to the genial glow of the fire, more
likely than not, the book being read will be by Mr.
Maxwell.   It might be a good definition of Mr. Maxwell,
to say that he was the novelist of the home, equally popu-

lar in the drawing room, as in the kitchen. And no
novelist can achieve to this eminence unless he is a great
artist. Mr. Maxwell is a great artist because he is a great
humanitarian, a great observer and a very wise commen-
tator.

Having generalised a little about Mr. Maxwell, we may
as well proceed to the particular and discuss in some detail
" The Day's Journey," that astounding study of two men.
Two men who quarrel, yet like each other, two men who
cannot keep away from each other, two men who can even
discuss one woman, two men who perhaps show us what
friendship really is.

When the two friends are discussing marriage Mr.
Maxwell works in a clever and sensible philosophy of it.
Not only that ; the dialogue between the two men, rather
contemptuous of marriage, yet intrigued by it, is a splendid
piece of understanding of the masculine mind.

> " ' It isn't a matter of thinking, Birdie. I know I
> shall never marry.'
>
> " ' Haven't you ever felt drawn to it ?' asked Bird ?
>
> " ' If I have, I've been quick to draw myself back in
> the opposite direction. No, to begin with, my temper
> is too uncertain for marriage—I mean, to make a
> woman consistently happy.'
>
> " ' Oh I wouldn't say that.'
>
> " 'And I have yet to meet a woman likely to make me
> consistently happy.' "

The for and against is wonderfully done. Mr. Maxwell
is a great master of dialogue, in which there is a striking
parallel to Mr. Walpole. The dialogue that is continued
between Bird and Heber gives us so much insight into the

extreme skill of Mr. Maxwell, that a further long quotation
serves a useful purpose.

> " ' No doubt, a good wife is in many respects the greatest
> comfort to a fellow, but a bad wife is the very devil.
> And the bother is you can never really know which sort
> you have not until you have married her, and then it is
> too late.   The thing that marriage takes from a bache-
> lor is his liberty.' "

Then we get the other side.   The masculine mind can
nearly always see two sides of a question, which is a reason
why it is quite often superior to the feminine mind.   The
feminine mind looks upon marriage (unconsciously perhaps) from the racial point of view, while the masculine
mind regards it from the individualistic point of view.
Women, for the most part, do not seem to be able to see
both sides with the facility of a man.   They see it if it is
pointed out specifically, but men see the other side spon-
taneously.   Thus there is the other side of marriage.   Bird
sums up delightfully.

> " ' On the other hand, an unmarried man when he
> gets old and finds himself without a wife and children is
> apt to feel a bit lonely.   His pals—the pals he was fond
> of—may have passed away.   He is then left alone in
> the world at the very time that he most needs com-
> pany.   To my mind, the whole thing is a matter of
> pro and con.   He must be one thing or the other.   He
> can't be both.'
> " ' Both what ?' asked Heber, whose thoughts had at
> last wandered.
> " ' Why a married man and a bachelor,' said Bird.

' I mean, he has to make his choice. And I personally choose the liberty—the freedom—the absence from worry.'

" ' So do I,' said Heber, getting up from his easy chair and stretching himself."

But Mr. Maxwell is a most skilful evolutionist, he knows well enough that the marriage question for the two old friends is not settled. The question never is settled, until a man has drawn his last breath. But get a woman over forty-five and she has told herself that marriage is not going to come her way. And the tragedy is that more often than not she is right in her assumption.

Thus these two confirmed old bachelors get into rather an uncomfortable position, when one of them falls desperately in love and having been ruthlessly turned down, the other does his best to put matters right. Here is the terrible letter that Heber writes to Bird, after the awful and tragic " turning down " by the lady he had hoped to marry. Again the skill of Mr. Maxwell as the dissector of the masculine mind is very apparent.

" Heber wrote : ' All is over. She has chucked me. These last days have felt blow about to fall. Fell yesterday evening. Shall join you to-morrow. Train Victoria 5.30. Reserve room.' "

When Bird goes to interview the detestable female, who has annihilated his friend's expected happiness, we get some delightful Maxwell irony and wit. A few lines taken at random may give some small idea of this. The situation is unique, one man interviewing a woman, to expostulate with her for refusing to marry his friend. Had ever man a more hopeless task?

This is the kind of conversation of which Bird delivers
himself.   It is all so natural, so ineffective, no man can
convince a woman that she has treated a man badly,
because she never thinks she has.   She only knows when
a man has treated *her* badly, she then whines and flies to
get legal assistance, so that being robbed of love she can
be compensated by mere pounds and a column in all the
cheap press.

" ' You had no right to lead him on.   You did lead
him on, you know.   And you had no right to do it.
When a man is not in earnest I say nothing against
leading him on—flirtation and so forth.   We all know
what that means.   But when you see that a man like
Wilfrid is in deadly earnest—and you cannot tell me
a girl does not detect at once—then I say you had no
right to take it as far as you did—practically to within
sight of the wedding day—and then throw everything
to the winds by intimating without warning that you
had changed your mind.' "

The result of the interview is not of course exactly en-
couraging as the only thing that Bird learns is that Miss
Glover is engaged to someone else.

The whole interview between Miss Glover and Bird is
one of the cleverest " sex" interludes that Mr. Maxwell
has ever written.   It brings out fundamentally the difference in viewpoint between the man and the woman
and shows with great truth and perception, that the
average woman, perfectly honest in money matters,
perfectly devoted to religion, perfectly virginal in matters
of sex, is in love diplomacy, cunning, quite unscrupulous
and never by any chance to be trusted.   And the indict-

ment is the more severe as Mr. Maxwell is never by any chance a cynic !

The effect on Heber of the finality of Miss Glover's determination not to marry him, is written by Mr. Maxwell with rare brilliance and faultless realism.

It shows that disappointment in love makes the rational man quite irrational. But disappointment in the case of a woman makes an irrational woman more often than not quite rational and eminently calm.

> " Heber was very bad after the revelation—worse, much worse than at any previous period. He refused food at ordinary meal times in the big coffee room, and would have sudden cravings for nourishment at impossible moments—when they were walking on the downs, from any place of entertainment, or late at night after the restaurant and the American bar were both closed."

Man is indeed inconsistent, he will swear that women have no place in his life, that he prefers the club to the fireside, that he is determined that no woman shall ask him why he is back so many hours after midnight, yet when a woman touches his jelly-like heart, he trembles with delight and when she finally throws his jelly-like heart under her feet, he wobbles like a shaking omnibus and cries out that life is over, all because of the woman that he swore would never take away his blessed bachelor liberty. How well does Mr. Maxwell bring it all out.

Possibly Mr. Maxwell's perfect command of his emotions is caused by his great ability for seeing two sides of a question. He has never so absorbed himself in one aspect of life, that the examination of that aspect has excluded all others. So many novelists only exploit a

particular view of life, it may be that they deal with
pleasant people and forget that there are unpleasant
people or (and this is much more frequent) they deal with
unpleasant people and forget that much of humanity is
pleasant. But Mr. Maxwell with a great amount of perception views life as a whole. In the discussion on marriage which I have been writing about which is found in
" The Day's Journey " we can see how Mr. Maxwell
looks " all round " a subject. It is, I think, a very
marked characteristic of all his work. And it is a characteristic that has a great deal to do with the value of Mr.
Maxwell as a novelist. Without any undue effort his
work is always on a high plane, we feel that he thinks
humanity is good at bed rock, an air of optimism blows
refreshingly about his pages.

Let us return to a further consideration of the two dear
old gentlemen in " The Day's Journey."

Again when the two old friends have married, one to a
rich woman, the other to a poor woman, Mr. Maxwell
writes delightfully of how the poor woman hates the rich
woman. Poor women often hate rich women, poor men
merely pity and secretly despise rich men. That is the
fundamental difference. A poor woman hates a rich
woman because she can have all the latest clothes, a poor
man despises a rich man because he knows that man is a
simple animal loathing the complexities that come with
riches.

Thus Bird's wife sums up her hatred of Mrs. Heber and
it is good reading because it is so true, because it shows
how women really loathe other women, merely on account
of silk stockings and fine hats. And you must know that
a poor woman hates a rich woman, when she comes to
visit her poor house, for rich women notice the accumula-

tion of dust, they notice that the coffee cups do not match, and unconsciously willing or unwilling, they show their feelings, and the poor woman is terribly hurt.   But rich men, though they also notice the uneven shapes and patterns of the coffee cups do not let others know that they have noticed.   Oh, yes, men are far cleverer than women and they never make poor people feel more poor, but rich women always do.   So Mr. Maxwell makes Mrs. Bird express her detestation of the rich Mrs. Heber.

> " ' What the devil does she mean by treating me as if I was dirt ?   And why do you let her do it ?   Coming into the drawing room in her overcoat—putting her hateful things on the piano—lolling on the arm of a chair—not caring if she breaks it.' "

" The Day's Journey " is a beautiful book written with an exquisite tenderness.   Mr. Maxwell has written good work since this book, he may write much more good work. But I do not think that he will again write " The Day's Journey."   I| do not think that a gigantic inspiration has the power to inspire the same writer, in the same way, twice.

And so I must turn to Mr. Maxwell when he is writing a completely different kind of book.

·   ·   ·   ·   ·   ·   ·

I have again taken a book of Mr. Maxwell's that is not one of his best known.   It is probably no part of this book to make any attempt to ask why certain books of an author are well known and certain are not, the difficulty of the problem is that quite often the least meritorious books of a writer are the best known.   This is not the

case with Mr. Maxwell but it is the case with many other
writers.   I suppose of all Mr. Maxwell's works " The
Guarded Flame " is his most widely known.   If I am
wrong in my assumption I rather think that it would be
wise to consider " The Devil's Garden " the best known.
At any rate it is the most tragic book that Mr. Maxwell
has written, it is a hideous tragedy because insanity and
murder are so closely allied in it.

Although I do not believe that it can be used as an
unalterable formula, quite often the least known books of
an author give most scope for a critical examination.

It is with this idea in my mind, that I proceed to discuss
in some detail Mr. Maxwell's delightful and eminently
homely book, " The Mirror and The Lamp."   A good deal
of this book has to do with that masterly grasp of describing the trivialities of life, which I have already said
is possessed by Mr. Maxwell to so extensive a degree.

It may be thought when I say that Mr. Maxwell pays
a great deal of attention to trivialities, that I mean he
deals with unimportant things.   I do not mean anything
of the kind.   Life is made up of trivialities, it is the trivial
acts that show character.   The reason that it is important
to consider the " trivialities " of Mr. Maxwell, is that they
are used to give a picture, in a book, of what life really is.
They are the small touches, which make the faithful
presentation.

I suppose to a certain extent the eating of a meal is a
triviality.   Yet the description of it makes us immediately
feel that we are reading of real life.   The smell of chops,
the atmosphere of fried fish, the pleasant pandemonium
of the family meal, with the pleasing flittering of the
" one of the family " servant, all this delicious homeliness
Mr. Maxwell conveys with elaborate skill.   Mr. Frankau

W. B. MAXWELL

by his descriptions of meals, makes us offensively hungry,
Mr. Maxwell not only makes us hungry, he makes us contented, for his meals are in the bosom of a family, that
exists behind every other closed door in our own unimportant yet divine street. Unimportant to the world but
divine to us, because the street is the channel by which we
reach our own home.

From " The Mirror and The Lamp " let me give a
quotation showing Mr. Maxwell describing a triviality,
but a triviality that breathes an intense homeliness and
a contented genial atmosphere.

> " In summer the Churchill boys did their " prepara-
> tion " at home and were not particular about supper ;
> but in winter they always went to evening school, and
> regularly brought back with them three hearty schoolboy
> appetites, the two elders especially made the cold meat
> and pickles fly. Maria, the staunch and trusted maid—
> to whom every liberty or privilege was permitted except
> that of giving notice to leave—freely commented on
> their voracious powers."

Then we get an absolutely ideal piece of homely dialogue, the kind of undistinguished conversation, that
happens in nearly every British home and could happen
no where else. It is all so natural, so easy, it all shows
how careful Mr. Maxwell is in the use of the right word and
the harmonious kind of chatter.

> " ' More mutton ?' she would say, affecting incredulity
> as Tom brought his plate once again to the sideboard.
> ' You astound me Mr. Thomas.' "

While we are on the subject of discussing the Maxwell

genius for writing of the family absorption of food, a slight
digression must be indulged in. I must leave " The
Mirror and The Lamp " and quote the best meal description that Mr. Maxwell has ever written. Mr. Maxwell is
indeed the autocrat of the supper table. It is a quotation
from " A Little More " that brilliant study of middle
class people. Those ~eople who are looked down upon
by the aristocracy and looked up to by the lower middle
class. Each class knowing that in reality England being
like a fish, the middle class is the backbone of it.

> " ' Some more soup ?' asked Mr. Welby.
> " ' No indeed, no,' said Mr. Carillon.
> " ' Miss Amabel ?'
> " ' No thank you, Mr. Welby.' "

Again a little later in the same meal. We have the
fatuous curate expostulating at his generous helping of
turbot. You will find such a curate in many homes in the
suburbs, for it is an uplift in the social scale to get the
curate, it is not everyone who can aspire to the extreme
dignity of feeding a vicar on turbot, and for most people
the spectacle of a bishop's teeth fastened in domestic turbot
is a wild impossibility !

> " ' Oh please don't help me too generously.'
> " ' Nonsense,' said Mr. Welby. ' At your age—with
> a hard day's work behind you.' "

Again the cleverness of Mr. Maxwell comes out. The
daughter must say something, for daughter's love curates,
it has nothing to do with religion, and nothing to do with
Christ, and nothing to do with the work of the Church, but
it has everything to do with social advancement. Why,

if you are the wife of a humble God-fearing commonplace little curate, you can visit the County people, and such a privilege is more than all the consolations of religion.

" ' And an evening service before you,' added Miss Violet, solicitously."

Still the same meal, Mr. Maxwell is taking us through in detail, and we have arrived at the mutton stage.   Again the whole small conversation is excellent, mutton in middle class suburbia always produces this kind of dialogue.

" Mr. Welby raised his voice, repeating the words loudly and rather severely :
" ' What follows ?'
" ' Roast mutton, sir,' replied the maid as she brought the plates.
" ' A leg, dear,' said Mrs. Welby."

Charming people are these that Mr. Maxwell writes of, to be found everywhere, perfectly commonplace, perfectly English, perfectly suburban, yet the backbone of The British Empire.

It is time that we returned to " The Mirror and The Lamp," the pleasant meal, into which we have wandered is over, and there are more serious matters to be considered.

.   .   .   .

It is a long way indeed from the homeliness of the supper table to the inmost thoughts of a young man, who is first enraptured by the thought, that he is to be the special servant of Christ.   In Mr. Maxwell's " The Mirror and

The Lamp " the thought comes to Churchill in the middle
of a moving hymn.   Perhaps nothing is so likely to appeal
to the ecstatic religious emotions as the music of a hymn,
the combination of sweet notes, the restfulness of an old
church, the half-hidden sanctity of the altar, the suggestion of adventure and mystery, the suggestion of leaving
the world and the flesh well alone, all these make their
strong appeal to the young man, who has felt the curious
call, that men define as Vocation.

This inward feeling that pervades Churchill is beautifully
and truthfully expressed by Mr. Maxwell.

" He thought of the grandeur of Christ and of His
courage.   He was braver than all the warriors the world
has ever seen.   He accepted death and torment at the
hands of those whom he had come to save.   He was the
Great Captain, the Hero of Heroes. What other leader
should a brave man want to follow ?"

Mr. Maxwell has exactly described what very young
men do feel, when they have an idea of being ordained,
the philosophical difficulties have not come in, the disturbing suggestion that crucifying God, is a little extrava-
gant, has perhaps not yet forced its unwelcome attention.
The thought that will come later, that a man may love a
woman's legs better than he loves Christ, has so far kept
in the background, that it is not yet seen.   Even the
worldly wish to serve Christ, as a bishop, rather than as
an unknown curate, probably does not worry the young
man, the adventure and implied sacrifice of the priestly
life seems all that matters.

What a skilful delineator of character is Mr. Maxwell,
his perception is uncanny and quite alarming.   We must

proceed a long way on, long after Churchill has been ordained, a delicate moment when he has to advise a woman about divorce. It is so easy for a priest to give the right advice when it affects someone else, all priests are admirable mechanical advice givers. Churchill speaks in the orthodox manner, the orthodox manner which assumes that it is the special interpreter of God.

> " He said it dully, yet with convincing firmness. As a Christian she must bear her cross. Divorce courts possessed no real power to set her free ; those whom God has joined together no man can sunder."

Of course man cannot, but it has never yet been proved that God cares, whether there is a marriage or whether there is not. It is a fact though, that many marriages are a curse, many divorces a blessing.

So we get to the end of the story. And it is a pitiful tragedy, because it shows how fatally ineffective the teaching of the priests really is. Churchill, the boy eager to serve the Christ, eager to tell the world that all marriages are until death, there can be no divorce, here is the tragedy, Churchill desperate for a woman, desperate for a divorce, desperate to give up everything for the possession of a woman's body. Once again, the body of a woman often has more power over a priest than the Body of Christ. Maxwell unsparingly writes the bald truth. It is naked, but it is quite unashamed

> " They sat on the wall, and, while he remained content with the present golden hours, she already spoke of the future—of the time when Robert Vickers should set her free and the Church could bless their union."

One of the main reasons why the Church has ever been served by those who cannot persist in her teachings, when the flesh comes in, is that the Almighty has so ordained it, that priests, like other men, will give up all their principles to gain an attractive woman. This, I think, is what Mr. Maxwell wishes to stress by " The Mirror and The Lamp." It must be a little disturbing, when a woman thinks about it, that she has more power over a man, whether he be priest or layman, than God has. Always provided of course that divorce is contrary to God's law. Mr. Maxwell has dealt with a melancholy subject, for whatever we may feel, we prefer to see a priest die in the faith for which he was ordained, than to see him renounce it all, to throw in his lot with a woman. It is indeed a pitiful exhibition, when the sacred rite of ordination cannot keep a man from the sexual snares of woman.

The fact of course that Mr. Maxwell makes Churchill comes back eventually to the Church proves nothing. The melancholy of the whole thing is that given sufficient temptation, a priest succumbs, his alleged special setting aside by God, seems to avail nothing. So I say that " The Mirror and The Lamp " is an undoubted tragedy.

.   .   .   .

There is a rare and refreshing grace about all Mr. Maxwell's work. Without being in the least puritanical, in the best sense, his fiction is pure, it is unadulterated by the close stink of filth or the far off vapour of unpleasant suggestiveness. Many present day novelists take infinite pains to expose the least agreeable side of life. If the public likes this tendency, and I believe it does, there is no conceivable reason for having any dislike of such fiction. I simply say that Mr. Maxwell does not *look* for unpleasantness, he does not shirk it, if it comes into his story, but there is no seeking after dirt, even if it be admitted that most fiction dirt to-day is very clever dirt.

To a certain extent Mr. Maxwell is on the side of sentimentalism, he appeals to the emotion that loves very dearly to enthuse over the long and rough road of love. But if Mr. Maxwell is sentimental, he is never sticky, he can write of a kiss with a sympathetic insight into the possibilities of sentiment that such an act may produce, but he does not write of a kiss as though it were a gallon jar of the most exquisite honey. You can get pretty deeply into the meshes of love, if you follow Mr. Maxwell, but he has no intention of allowing his readers to wallow. As I have said or hinted before, he keeps a very admirable control over himself.

Mr. Maxwell has a most remarkable power again, of delving into horror, not so much rough external horror, as internal gnawing relentless horror. And this internal horror is infinitely more horrible than external horror. "The Devil's Garden" is a splendid story of a growing horror, the terrible fact that a murderer cannot escape his own conscience, that if he escapes the quick gallows drop, he will undergo the more depressing gradual evolution from sanity to insanity.

Perhaps in some ways Maxwell is the most delicate writer of fiction that we can find at the present moment. And when I say he is delicate, I mean he is delicate because he is strong and not because he is weak. Delicate literary strength is not caused by any weakness or fear of ugliness, it is caused by a certainty, by a strength, by a feeling that life is so brittle, so liable to break where it is least expected, that it must be dealt with in a delicate manner.

Mr. Maxwell is, if we may put it this way, always *kind* to the characters he creates, he writes of them in almost a sorrowing way when they fail, he writes of them with genuine joy, when they succeed. The same genial kindly smile, with which Mr. Maxwell greets those who have had the privilege of meeting him, can be found in his pages. There is nothing harsh about Maxwell, if he is sometimes severe, he is severe in almost a fatherly way.

Many Americans have said that Maxwell is great. America is usually right in what she says, if she is likely to be wrong she does not say it. Maxwell is great, he is great because he is a very careful novelist and nothing he writes is not well worth reading. The combination of his varied gifts, his humour, his pathos, his sympathy, his command of tragedy, his controlled sentimentality, all these have made him great.

Like most writers of the first rank, Maxwell is at infinite pains to use the most appropriate word. In an almost old-fashioned way at times he writes long blocks of solid description, yet it is all done so well, that the block *seems* short.

Maxwell is interested in humanity, because he knows that humanity is first of all interested in humanity, and humanity is the mass that makes or breaks the novelist. But never does Maxwell write for effect, on the other hand, his writing is always effective. What it obviously sets out to do, it does. It sets out primarily to tell a good story and secondly to indicate something ethical and both these ambitions are always thoroughly satisfied. Maxwell writes his books meaning them to be successful and in every way they are eminently successful.

Possibly that much misunderstood word " stylist " can be used of Maxwell.   Not that Maxwell is "nice" or even a pedant, he is a stylist in that he makes his words do their proper duty, that is they convey exactly the impression they are meant to convey.   Maxwell is not in any sense " precious," that word which so many Oxford and Cambridge young *asses* of both sexes like to use about literary men, who are as careful as Maxwell most indubitably is.

No one I suggest can read Maxwell without experiencing a sense of really keen enjoyment, and the taste left in the mouth is a pleasurable one.   I should not care to say that Maxwell has any new theory of the world or any particular idea as to how the whole course of human progress might be bettered.   His problems are practical ones, his people are the ordinary people we might meet in any house.   A good deal of his atmosphere is " indoors."

Reading Maxwell, we experience the warm glow of the fire, the pleasant atmosphere of the domestic meal, the love adventures of young men and young maidens.   Yet also ; reading Maxwell we can shiver at an atrocious murder, we can shudder (a deeper form of shivering) at the gradual making of a madman.

It has often been said that simplicity is akin to greatness, not that they are always interchangeable.   Maxwell is both simple and great and the combination have produced a novelist who is a brilliant artist and a sincere realist.

END OF PORTRAIT FIVE

PORTRAIT NUMBER SIX
I A N   H A Y

PORTRAIT NUMBER SIX

IAN HAY

THERE is nothing in life so sweet and charming as something that is really young. Most people to-day are never young, except when they are growing really old. It is then that they see that youth is not a matter of years but a matter of outlook.

Why is it that people say quite generally and quite often, that the days of school are the best ? Not because life then is necessarily joyful, not because it is the beginning of a grand adventure, but rather because the age of school is the age of youth. It is the age when the sky is still blue, the heavens are very clear, the goal is very certain, the world is very small, the honours that school can give are more precious than all the honours that life can give after. A man may become the Archbishop of Canterbury, but it will not thrill him, as the morning he first heard, and hardly believed, that his name was one of the school eleven. A man may witness great sorrow in his life, but he will never more than once experience the deadening blow, when the cold, callous newspaper contains the official and deplorable obituary of his old headmaster. And perhaps the joy and sorrow that I have mentioned spring from the same source, that the entry into the school eleven and the remembered contact with the headmaster, happened when the man was young, when the school cap covered the place that later held a bowler, when the man thought more of the tuck shop than all the deadly and melancholy splendour of the great hotels that flourish in the great cities, that men and women may eat and be quickly filled ere they are whirled away to lie with the poor worms of the earth.

Ian Hay is more than anything else the novelist of glorious youth. In his writings, he has brilliantly captured the essential abandon and divinity of being young. In an age of old young men and older young women, Ian Hay stands out as the determined writer, who will write of youth, of life at school and just out of it. He is the novelist who delights in the exuberance of boys, it is of the embryo man that he makes a book. Without any apology whatever I shall devote the whole of this Essay to a discussion on the delightful work of Ian Hay's which he has called, with infinite wisdom, " Pip."

.   .   .   .

It is rather a curious thing, that in a book dealing with youth, there should be found very early, a note of melancholy. The note of melancholy is not experienced by Pip but it is experienced by his father. It is always melancholy for a father to look at his son, because the young boy, or the squawking infant, reminds that the years are growing heavy and their weight more and more noticeable.

But Ian Hay is not content with the normal melancholy that fathers undergo, it is the abnormal and gnawing melancholy, when the father gazes at his son, and knows that the mother who bore him, has long passed out of sight. This piece of the sad side of life, as I say, comes in

early in " Pip " and Ian Hay writes of it delicately and
with admirable taste.   It is worth quoting for Ian Hay,
though he can write of laughter so that we feel the world
is but the reflection of the sun, can also write so that we
feel the world might easily be drowned in the tears of its
sorrowing inhabitants.

" After the children had gone Father staring at his
untasted dinner.   Occasionally his gaze travelled to
the opposite end of the table, where someone used to
sit—someone who had been taken from him by an
inscrutable Providence five years before."

Ian Hay is right in his word " inscrutable " but perhaps
really man is more inscrutable than God.   With regard to
life and death, Providence seems to take a vicious delight
in the violent process of severance and Ian Hay may well
indeed use the tactful word " inscrutable."

Ian Hay seems to have a very remarkable understanding
of school life, not only the actual life of the boys but the
actual processes of emotions which crowd in upon the
schoolboy.   No creature is more difficult to analyse.
The schoolboy is absolutely unreasonable, irrational, he is
both tender and cruel, he has a contempt for anything that
is more " new " than himself, his school is the world and
in the early days his " world " is a far larger and more
terrifying place, than all the real world he moves about in,
in later years.   Probably the first day at school is the
most dreadful in the whole life of any man, it is a barbarous
transition from the exaggerated humanity of the home, to
the seeming inhuman savagery of the school.   Boys may
weep because they see their mother's driven rapidly away
from the schoolgates, but they would if they dared scream

with terror at the atrocities which await them in the dormitory, the land where new boys first learn the dreadful inhumanity of humanity to humanity.

For let it be thoroughly remembered by those who say schooldays are the best days, that they say this when the schooldays, if not " forty years on," are a good many years on. As a race schoolboys, with few exceptions, are by instinct pernicious little cads, only the dread of the prefects and the greater dread of the masters and the greatest dread of the headmaster gives some sort of order to the communistic and oligarchical mass of humanity which is to be found in every school. Whether the same thing applies to girls is a doubtful question. But probably the race of schoolgirls are much more civilised than their male contemporaries.

Pip's first day at school is well expressed. Ian Hay comments on the sudden size that Pip's world has become. For when we go to school, for good or evil, we go out into the world, and we do not again go out of the world until we finally do go out of the world into the silence which is more complete than all the vast silences of The Arctic wastes.

" Mr. Evans having made a dignified exit, the children for the first time in their lives, found themselves alone in the world and suddenly realised that the world was very big and they were very small."

This is indeed well put. We all feel that the world is very large, it is so large that we are lost in its mazes, yet it is so small that we have passed through, ere we are conscious that the journey is ending. And the peculiar thing is, that most of us think that we are immortal, we laugh, dance, and waste the hours, while watching us is the dread angel of death and his smile has veiled malice.

But for the time being the world about which we are writing is a confined world, it is the delightful universe that Ian Hay has created, in which Pip plays his pure and honest part. For " Pip " is the story of a great success, not a worldly success which is measured by money and titles, but a success in life, when the word success denotes grim determination, undaunted courage and above all a quiet resignation to hard and uncongenial times.

Ian Hay introduces us to a good deal of the behind the scenes in a school, far from the " dishonesty " of speech days, far from the purring speeches by which parents are so easily beguiled.

There is no good denying the unpleasant fact that public schools and private schools are very largely permeated by a spirit of favouritism. Masters, quite naturally prefer the brilliant boys, they bring more credit to the school, they are better advertisements and in modern times the average headmaster's chief concern is how to advertise his school. - I am afraid that it is no exaggeration to say that most masters and most headmasters care little about the dull boys, they have little or no conception that the person who should be worried about is the dull boy, the boy who wins no scholarships, the boy who never receives any prizes, the boy who occupies an inferior position in the school. But instead, the dull boy crouches at the back of the class, he understands little he is told, the masters hate him, because it is the acme of misery to drill facts into a head that is absolutely wooden. The dull boy hates the masters, he feels he is despised, that no added glory to the school will be brought about through him. The brilliant boy is the pet of the masters, it is he who will set the glory of the school in a crown of gold, and the brilliant boy likes the masters, for he knows rightly enough, that they are on his side.   I do not believe that one headmaster in a hundred cares for anything except the clever boys, his only concern is to get enough dull boys to make his school financially possible.

Although he puts the matter somewhat diffidently, Ian Hay has some idea of the antagonism that exists between master and boys when he writes :

" Nearly every schoolboy has a *bête noire* among the masters, and every master has at least one *bête noire* among the boys."

Ian Hay then continues, and his sentiments are, I think, untrue.   For he says :

" Fortunately it is very seldom that the antipathy is mutual."

The antipathy which exists between certain masters and certain boys is nearly always mutual.   Dislike has a supreme habit of passing from one individual to another and back.   It is only in the matter of sex that one loves and the other dislikes.   When a boy dislikes a master, the master reciprocates the emotion.   Of course the boy cannot actively show his dislike of the master in the same way that the master can very actively demonstrate his state of non-affection for the boy.   But I think that in ninety per cent. of cases, dislike between boys and masters is mutual to the detriment of the respective functions of both.

Ian Hay gives a delicious description of the entrance of

the headmaster when the boys are in the middle of a kind of " rag " of an unpopular master. The writing is clever, for Ian Hay is not writing a book for boys, but a book about a boy, and it is for grown up people, and grown up people will chuckle with huge delighted chuckles at the scene Ian Hay paints.

" After his usual punctilious knock—he was a headmaster of the velvet glove type—he opened the door, and stood an interested and astonished spectator of the scene within."

Headmasters are always astonished and their astonishment is such that the school boy beholding it feels that life can be more of terror than he had anticipated. We never fear anyone as we fear our headmaster, and we never love anyone as we love him when we have left. Meet the " head " at an old boy's dinner, hear him speak to his now full-grown " boys " and you will know the subtle indefinable link that makes an old boy always reverance his headmaster.

" On the benches rolled thirty boys, helpless, speechless, tearful with laughter ; and upon the rostrum, with a parti-coloured bald head and a coal black face, there mowed and gibbered a creature, which rolled frenzied eyes and gnashed unnaturally whitened teeth in impotent frenzy upon the convulsed throng before him."

And the climax is glorious, it can only once be experienced in life and the memory is a blessed one right down to the end of all things.

" Linklater had covered the door-handle with lamp-black and Mr. Bradshaw's favourite mannerism had done the rest."

.   .   .   .

I should not be a bit surprised if Ian Hay does not know a great deal more about boys than those very learned and well meaning people who spend so much time considering the question of adolescence. A very perplexing question is the one of boy love. It is a peculiar muddle of emotions, the boy quite suddenly is precipitated into the vague and rather terrifying realisation that he is a person of sex and that in the world are other beings, mysterious, inscrutable, producing in him fears, longings and qualms that he cannot interpret, for the very good reason that there is no interpretation. Sex though it is universal is individual, it is inherent and it comes and shakes the unprepared boy viciously.

The boy, when he falls in love is the prey of an emotion which delights and yet worries him at the same time. I have already said that Ian Hay knows a great deal about boys, and he knows how to write sympathetically about them. I rather think that one of the best passages that his pen has yet produced is the one in " Pip " which deals with the first love of a boy for a girl, that straightforward emotion which has none of the hateful attributes of love in after life, as marrying for position, marrying to please match-making, detestable old mothers. Ian Hay is full of sympathy for the love that the boy experiences and he is of the opinion that the process should be considered seriously. We make fun of the boy who falls in love, because we have long forgotten that first love is the most intense for the time being of all love, we laugh at the poor deluded youth, we tell him it will wear off, it is like measles we tell him that what matters is not the girl over the way, but the honour of the house eleven, we have forgotten that the youthful rapture of first love never comes again. We have forgotten that it has passed for ever, the street is empty, the girl we loved when we were very young, will never walk down our street again. If we passed her, we should not know her, we are terribly grown up, the angel we had thought so wonderful, is only an ordinary commonplace woman, but you grown ups, you have so easily smashed a divine dream.

It is a terrible thing to be grown up for we are the arch criminals who smash the ideals of boyhood, it is we who sneer at the enthusiasm of youth, it is we who are cynical over the " calf love " of boyhood. But we should with Ian Hay consider most carefully the whole question of boy love. His discussion is so important, so admirable, so full of understanding, that a long quotation has every right to its prominent place in this Essay.

" Now, roughly speaking, a man is in love from his fifteenth birthday onwards ; nature has ordained it. But in most cases civilisation, convention, society— call it what you like—has ordained that he must not treat this, the most inspiring passion of human life, as anything more than a jest for another ten years or so. And therein lie more little tragedies—disintegrated castles in the air, secret disappointments and endless efforts of of self repression—than this world dreams of."

Ian Hay contrasts the happy position of the girl with the unhappy position of the boy. It is of course merely the conventional inanity that girls ought to love early in life, boys ought not.

The origin of such an assumption may be found in the fact that history has determined that man shall be the individual to go out and conquer the universe, while woman shall stay at home and make the homes of the universe.

" Contrast with this the happy case of the girl. If she chooses to fall in love at the age of eighteen nothing is deemed prettier or more natural ; she is at liberty to enjoy her birthright openly ; she receives sympathetic assistance on every hand ; and if at the age of nineteen or twenty she decides to marry, society comes and sheds rapturous tears at the wedding."

With considerable wisdom Ian Hay though he considers boy love a serious matter, realises that boy and girl marriages would not be useful or possible in society as it is at present constituted.

" Of course boy and girl marriages would never do. Joint inexperience is a sure guarantee of disaster. Still, sentimental persons may be permitted one sigh of regret for a millennium which, however idyllic and unpractical it might be, would at anyrate prevent young men from marrying wealthy widows and pretty girls from giving themselves, in exchange for a position in society, to middle aged gentlemen with five figure incomes."

Perhaps the matter is at present inevitable, dreams must be shattered, high castles must fall in a chaotic heap, the sun must be obscured, the flowers must wither and die but at least we can determine with Ian Hay.

" If a young man must spend the best years of his
life in repressing his tenderest instincts, let us at any
rate refrain from laughing at his struggles."

Ian Hay writes with considerable acumen concerning
the homage that Pip feels ought to be paid to women.
Most boys feel this homage, for knowing nothing whatever
about women, they imagine them to be spotless, tender,
full of compassion, long suffering ; later they learn that
instead women are full of guile, value a man in pounds
shillings and pence, have cultivated almost to the rank of
genius the art of deception and altogether are, what they
ever have been, not angels or devils, but sex attractors,
that the race may continue.   The race may much depend
on evolution, but the birth rate largely depends on
women's legs and women are quite aware of this, conse-
quently most women look upon a man as something to
be captured.   But Ian Hay writes what the ordinary boy
thinks of a girl and he writes extraordinarily truly.

" Pip regarded women in general much as the poor
Indian regards the sun, moon, and other heavenly
bodies—as things not to be understood or approached,
but merely to be worshipped."

Is it not indeed a tragedy that boys should worship false
gods ?
A little later Ian Hay shows how miserably Pip mis-
understands women.   For, say what you will, women
hate to be treated with an elaborate courtesy, for unconsciously this depicts sex disability, and certain inferiority.
So, evidently the girls of Pip's acquaintance are a little
bored by his politeness.

" He treated all women, from his sister's friends to the most plebeian young person who ever dispensed refreshments across a bar, with a grave courtesy which the more frivolous members of that captious sex occassionally found rather full."

All boys should be taught to be polite to women in a matter of degree. The greatest politeness should be shown to a charwoman, the politeness shown to a duchess need not be so marked, for the charwoman will be grievously hurt if you are rude, but the duchess will merely be sorry for you, if you are not polite to her !

The several quotations I have given have been included to prove that Ian Hay has a masterly understanding of the mind of the boy. In fact I do not know of a novelist of the present day who has a larger understanding of the boy than Ian Hay. Pip is absolutely true to life, he can be found in any school, his outlook is that of ninety per cent. of youths.

Not only does Ian Hay completely understand the boy, he also completely understands the relations between a father and his son. There is nothing so curious as the relation between a father and his son. The son is shy of his father, the father is far more shy of his son. Yet in most cases a perfect sympathy exists between the two. Where it does not, there is impending tragedy, the type of dire misery that is to be found in Mr. Walpole's " Fortitude." The one thing that the average boy is afraid of showing in front of his father is any emotion, the one thing that the father is terrified of showing in front of his son, is any outward emotion. Few fathers will dare to do more than shake hands with their sons, when the days of school have begun. You must kiss your son before he has gone

IAN HAY

into the world of school, for after you will never do this
thing again.

There is a very remarkable piece of dialogue when Pip
discusses with his father the unpleasant fact that he will
never have enough brains to qualify for the medical profession.   On such a delicate subject, Ian Hay brings out
the whole position with astonishing skill.   It is the kind
of heart to heart talk which is always taking place in all
sorts of houses, while outside, unheeding, the population
hurries by on its multitudinous affairs.

> " ' And who is going to do my work ?'
> " ' I wish I could,' said Pip impulsively for him.
> ' Dad, I must be a devil of a disappointment to you.
> Fancy you and me.' "

It is very difficult to say who experiences the greater
disappointment.   The son, who is not as much a success
as the father had hoped, or the father who finds his son is
not going to do anything at all remarkable, even if he
attains to any profession at all.   Ian Hay writes of this
sort of question well.

> " ' We don't all get ten talents, old man,' said his
> father.   ' But soon I daresay, when you are qualified,
> there will be lots . . .'
> " Pip put down his glass of port.
> " ' Dad, I shall never be qualified,' he said.
> " ' Why ?'
> " ' Because I haven't got it in me.   You are so clever
> that you can't conceive what a fool's brain can be like.
> I tell you honestly that thing is beyond me, governor.
> I have worked pretty hard . . .'
> " ' I know that,' said his father heartily."

The confession is naturally a blow, no man likes his
flesh and blood to be a failure, it is a sad climax and Ian
Hay measures the extent of it truly.

> " He had been a lonely man all his life, and now
> especially that his health was uncertain, he realised the
> unhappy fact that his son—his big, strong, healthy son,
> to whose intellectual companionship he had looked
> forward so eagerly was never to give him a shoulder to
> lean on save in a physical sense."

From what I have said it may appear that Ian Hay only
excels in the drawing of a boy and a young man.   I do
not wish to imply anything of the kind.   It is only
natural that in a story that concerns school life so largely,
not too much attention is given to women.

But towards the end of the book, when Pip has lost his
father, when Pip is a workman in a motor works, we get a
good piece of feminine outlook, when Pip (unwise hero)
ventures to suggest to a woman that marrying a rich
husband, not for himself, but for his riches is not exactly
first class cricket.   The retort that the female makes is
delightful, for men must never talk morals to women, they
hate it, they may have to put up with it from a bishop but
from a mere layman, and a young one, never.

> " ' Women were never meant for that low down sort
> of game,' said Pip, getting to the heart of his subject."

As if any woman ever thought that *her* game was low
down, what a lot of the masculine mind must consist of
pulp !

" Suddenly Lottie blazed out.

" ' There you go! Women, women, women! I wonder if there was ever a man in this world that could treat a woman sensibly. Some men—most men—look upon women as fair game, and treat them accordingly. The others—men like you—look on them as little pot angels, and shudder when they show they are made of flesh and blood.' "

Then Lottie tells us what women really are, but we shall not believe her, for we know a woman never means what she says !

" ' Women are human beings, no better and no worse than men, only they don't get the chances men do, Jack. That's all—human beings ! Remember that.' "

But Ian Hay is perhaps now a little out of date when he makes Lottie say " they don't get the chances men do," for women to-day get all the chances that men get, the only difference is that they take them more readily. Ian Hay well understands the sudden inexplicable moods of women, moods which bewilder a man, and leave him gaping and feeling a fool and wishing that he had not considered any logic a part of woman's mental equipment.

" The irregularity of the situation apparently struck Miss Lottingar at the same moment, for with one of those swift and characteristically feminine changes of mood which leave mere man toiling helplessly behind in the trammels of logical consistency, she abruptly released her arm, observed brightly that the rain had ceased, wondered if it wouldn't turn out a fine evening, and bade Armstong drive home as fast as possible."

There is a glorious finish to " Pip," for it is of that moment, when the wind sighes a soft lullaby, the clouds seem to drop a gentle blessing, the grass is greener than we had thought it could be, the flowers have a scent that reaches our nostrils like a sweet perfume from an Eastern bazaar, because by our side, is a girl, and this girl, the apex to us of all womanhood, has said, shyly, almost inaudibly, that it is we who have won, we who have the right to be the pilot until life ends.

" Once she said . . .
" ' Pip you're getting awfully wet.'
" Pip looked down upon her for a moment.　Then he looked up again and shook his glistening head defiantly at the weeping heavens.
" ' Who cares ?' he roared."

Who cares, who cares, watchman of our fates, we heed you not, all is well, who cares, who cares.

.　　.　　.　　.　　.　　.　　.

Ian Hay's output has not, up to the present, been particularly big in quantity, but it has always been big in quality.　The art of the novelist, for Ian Hay, is the art of telling a pleasant story, and at the same time adding many wise and searching comments.　It is impossible to find any nasty eroticism in his writings, Ian Hay writes of a clean world, and it is so much more useful to write of a clean world rather than a dirty world.　Unless of course (and many novelists do this) a dirty world is written of, with the intention of trying to make it cleaner.　But this is perhaps to make the main function of the novelist, that of an instructor, and probably this is subjecting the

province of fiction to an unfair task. Ian Hay does
instruct, I have shown his instruction in one or two
" comment " quotations from " Pip " but his ideal is to
write a straightforward story, as true to life as possible,
yet avoiding any too deep or searching psycho-analysis.
The study of a character by Ian Hay is a totally different
bit of art to study of character by Miss Sinclair. Both are
very high in their conceptions, but they are different.

It would have been with the greatest pleasure that I
should have said something about Ian Hay's supremely
fine work about the great war. But it is outside the
province of this book and I must reluctantly refrain.
Perhaps what fiction needs very sorely to-day is the type of
work of Ian Hay. I do not think that it will get it, for
people like to dig very deeply, they like to see sex, not
through their own eyes, but through the microscopic eye
of the novelist. The simple tale of Ian Hay is *not yet* the
general order of the day. Possibly Ian Hay has not the
extreme powers of examination that could make him
write the deeply philosophical novels of a Bennett or a
Wells. Yet, if this is not so, his work is always wanted
and wanted desperately by a humanity which is beginning
to ask ; is there *anything* in the world that matters except
divorce and marriage intricacies ?

At present I do not believe that Ian Hay has written
the book that will go down to posterity, yet if we frankly
ask this question, who can really dare to say what will go
down. Of all the miracles, the miracle of literary perma-
nence and literary " death " is the most mysterious and
the most likely to upset our carefully thought out pro-
phecies.

Most novelists of our own time have remarkable powers
of writing dialogue and Ian Hay is not an exception to the

general rule. His style is easy and attractive. On the
whole he seems to have an optimistic outlook on life.
Though sorrows creep in, laughter and joy, are more the
order of the day. Ian Hay does not seem to trouble
particularly with problems, he has no ready conception of
philosophical fiction. He has a very fair amount of imagi-
nation but his supreme quality is the delightful freshness
and buoyancy of his writings.

There are those who would possibly hardly class Ian
Hay as a novelist at all but rather the teller of several
pleasing stories. There is a subtle difference in the distinction, but it is too pedantic to merit serious attention.
There are naturally many grades in the novel, and the
grade that Ian Hay occupies is perchance the grade which
contains fiction of a purely story telling nature. Yet,
as I have already said, Ian Hay has his serious moments,
he reflects, but he does not primarily use the novel as
propaganda or even as the " solver " of social and meta-
physical problems. But, if we use the word novelist, in
the popularly accepted sense, that it is a story and something that is new, then Ian Hay is a novelist of a high
position. And I think the novelist is fundamentally the
teller of a tale; the problem story, the intimate character
study, these are but additions to the main function of the
novel.

So we may leave it that Ian Hay is a first class teller of
a pleasant story and in spite of the varied meanings that
are now attached to the word novel, I am content to say
that Ian Hay is a talented and clever novelist.

END OF PORTRAIT SIX

PORTRAIT NUMBER SEVEN
REBECCA WEST

PORTRAIT NUMBER SEVEN
REBECCA WEST

IT must be obvious to anyone who reads the work of Miss West that in her is to be found what I may call a germ of grim brilliancy. She is brilliantly conversant with the more serious side of life. Miss West writes as if she was rather angry with humanity, as if she viewed the mass of people amongst whom she moves and has her being with a slightly malicious smile. Perhaps at present, and I say this advisedly, (for Miss West is comparatively young), she cannot see the sun because the clouds obscure it, yet she would do well to remember that though not seen the sun is still there. Miss West has of course had a remarkable success in a comparatively short literary career and in every way she deserves it, for if Miss West is as yet somewhat uncertain of her own feet and much more certain of the feet of other people, she has every chance of a most distinguished career in the world of letters. But Miss West would do very well to be beware of the newspapers. Lately she has written many superficial articles, in which she attacks men, in an extremely cheap kind of way. Miss West is too good an artist, she has too brilliant gifts, she has too great powers of really fine writing, to develop into a kind of woman, to whom the Editors of the cheaper press write, when they wish to secure an article that is merely written to cause correspondence.

Miss West's own work is her own publicity, there is no need for her to seek it by making " smart " statements to interviewing reporters. Miss West is by nature a literary woman, her splendid study of Henry James is proof enough of this, but she does not appear to have any marked journalistic qualities, her brain is perhaps a little too acute and possibly too finely moulded to make a good writer of articles which merely interest for the fraction of a moment and die never to share in the joy of resurrection. Literature may always expect to share in a resurrection, but journalism seldom if ever does so. It is of course true that certain journalistic articles are resurrected to become a book, but that is a birth or a new birth from journalism into literature and not a journalistic resurrection.

Miss West is so great an artist and so sincere, that it would be a thousand pities if she spent much time in writing the kind of journalism that is written by society women, chorus girls and other members of the female sex whose intelligence, while sharp and even smart, is by no means profound. For Miss West is a very profound writer when she likes, she can make men and women ponder, she has remarkable powers of insight in certain directions and extraordinary superficial qualities on the other. I give an example. It is melancholy to find that a woman who can produce such a work of extreme distinction as " The Judge " should allow it to be reported of her in a morning journal that she said " I like to see men in a subordinate position, that is all they are fit for." Now, no one wishes to interfere with what Miss West feels about men, in fact but a very few would in the least care, but anyone who was delighted to see the making of a brilliant writer like Miss West, would be distressed to hear her utter an inanity such as " that is all they are fit for."

Miss West has made a great name, she can do and has done fine work, but unless she is careful to keep a check on what she says and writes in the public press, we shall be the spectators of an unfortunate dualism in one woman, a brilliant literary artist and a " smart " and superficial journalist.

But I must turn to the special business of this Essay, a discussion on the book by which Miss West has attained a large part of her fame which is called by the grim and rather depressing title of "The Judge."

.   .   .   .

It is rather appropriate that Miss West should start her fine story " The Judge " in a grim atmosphere. For the story is a grim story, it frowns and thunders, it has no trace of geniality, it is stark staring realism, it is the tragic side of life that is written of and the story starts in the grim city of Edinburgh. I love Edinburgh, I love the cold inhumanity of its magnificent castle, I love the way the city frowns cynically at the crowds carelessly shopping and gossiping in Princes Street, I love the clear cutting biting winds that tear through Edinburgh and whirl into the corners and round the houses as though the wind loves this city so much, it must hurry lest it be kept a willing prisoner. But Edinburgh is a grim city, it is the entrance town to the grim north, it is unemotional, Edinburgh is the home of great causes and the grim mother of ardent pioneers.

And it is this great city of the far north that Miss West takes us when she introduces an ardent feminist, one Miss Melville and " she was a suffragette, so far as it is possible to be a suffragette effectively when one is just seventeen,

and she spent much of her time composing speeches which
she knew she would always be too shy to deliver."

Perhaps this is almost the keynote to the whole of " The
Judge " for Miss Melville is really a rather ineffective
person, being entirely concerned that she should be
effective. This is probably the underlying tragedy of
" The Judge." There is nothing in this world more
depressing, more hopeless, than the type of person, who
feels that he could do so much and yet achieves so little.
Witness poor Miss Melville selling a paper dealing with
Votes for Women in Princes Street, selling to the unheeding mass of fat and thin human beings, too intent on
securing Sunday meat for their miserable bellies, to take
any interest in questions of political rights for women.
How wonderfully Miss West gets the "atmosphere" of the
cold callous and detestable humanity which flows along a
great public street, giggling girls, fat satisfied and salacious
looking women, leering men and lewd youths, how Miss
West hates them, and she is right in her hatred, for mass
humanity is an excrescence and a pulsating mass of selfish
desires. Well, may Miss West feel pessimistic, these
passers-by care for nothing but their miserable puny little
selves and poor Miss Melville may stand and watch the
mob flow by, the flotsam and jetsam of any great city.

" It seemed the height of folly to work for the race if
the race was like this : men who, if they had dignity,
looked cold and inaccessible to fine disastrous causes ;
men who were without dignity and base as monkeys ;
mountainous old men who looked bland because the
crevices of their expressions had been filled up with fat,
but who showed in the glares they gave her and her
papers an immense expertness in coarse malice ; hen-

like genteel women with small mouths and mean little figures that tried for personality and all other adornments irrelevant to the structure of the human body; flappers who swung scarlet bows on their plaits and otherwise assailed their Presbyterian environment by glad cries of the appearance ; and on all these faces the smirk of superior sagacity that vulgar people give to the untriumphant ideal."

This is indeed bitter writing, it displays in no small measure a personality that might easily be termed disagreeable. But much *more* does it postulate a personality that is disappointed, disgusted and appalled at the appalling lack of any interest that humanity takes in big questions. It is always the same, the public outlook is always suburban, gossip is preferred to sound conversation, the people is so credulous that it will worship local tin gods, listen to their vain and bleating trumpetings, while outside, great men and great women manufacture great causes, but only the few listen, and the vast mob rushes by intent on meat and grub and sordid gain.

On a purely literary question, shall I find fault with Miss West because she has apparently no conception of the art of compression ? I ask the question for I am not sure whether compression is a virtue or a vice. There is a considerable movement in present day fiction towards compression, the use of the asterisks fulfil many strange and hitherto undreamed of functions. On the other hand, with a writer like Miss West, every possible word that she can use, she does, and she uses a great deal too many. The solid blocks of very close print in which Miss West indulges are not only extremely irritating but tend to obscure the meaning. Probably, as in most other things,

the middle course is the best.   A certain amount of compression and a certain amount of expansion.   I give an
example of what I call the unnecessary verbiage of Miss
West, the whole description is tiring, the brain is wearied
in its attempts to follow the detailed intricacies.   The
description of Yaverland is much too detailed, it makes us
feel that we should pray hard never to be allowed to gaze
upon a man in whom could be found so many identification
marks.   Miss West describes Yaverland as if she was writing a learned treatise on anatomy, only it is not nearly so
useful.

" His black hair lay in streaks and rings on his rain-
wet forehead and gave him an abandoned and magical
air, like the ghost of a drowned man risen for revelry ;
his dark gold skin told a traveller's tale of far off pleasurable weather ; and the bare hand that lay on his knee
was patterned like a snake's belly with brown marks,
doubtless the stains of his occupation."

We have to read a passage like this two or three times
to gather clearly the impression that Miss West wishes to
convey.   Compression in this kind of word painting would
not only be a virtue, it would be a matter of utility.
There is something even nauseating in this intimate picture, especially as it is supposed to be what Miss Melville
saw in her contemplation of Yaverland.   With such a
penetrating glance, the logical outcome, given opportunity, must be fornication, which in spite of being deadly
is a most popular sin.

A little later Miss West is again nauseating in her consideration of the female shape of the body.   It is not of
course surprising that Yaverland noticed that Miss Melville

" was made like a delicate beast ; in the valley between her high small breasts there lay a shadow, which grew greater when she breathed deeply."

But we do not need all these details, the interest to the casual reader, in the matter of Miss Melville, is not the contour of her breasts or the delightful suggestion of her body but the trend of her brain. Having told us that Yaverland noticed that Miss Melville had " a valley between her high small breasts " Miss West immediately informs us that Yaverland " looked at her with the dispassionateness which comes to men who have lived much in countries where nakedness offers itself unashamed to the sunlight."

The connection between observation of women's breasts and masculine dispassionateness is a strange kind of logic and can hardly be considered as being usual.

But perhaps one of the functions of fiction at the present day is to deal with problems and Miss West has some extraordinarily good things to say about illegitimate children, about whom there is more hypocrisy than about any other social problem.

We find that Miss Melville (and why does Miss West make her possessed of such meagre intelligence?) is at a feminist meeting in Edinburgh and is indignant at the treatment of illegitimate children.

" Ellen clapped loudly, not because she had any great opinion of unmarried mothers, whom she suspected of belonging to the same type of woman who would start on a day's steamer excursion and then find she had forgotten the sandwiches, but because she was a neat-minded girl and could not abide the State's pretence that an illegitimate baby had only one parent when everybody knew that every baby had really two."

But surely a girl of the mentality that Miss West makes Miss Melville would not be much good to the feminist cause, for Miss Melville continues ruminating in this way and it is absurdly unreal. It is quite remarkable how Miss West descends suddenly from reason to non-reason.

" Children, she was sure, came into the world because of some kind of embrace."

If this is the mentality of many young women, it is surprising that there are so few illegitimate children in the world. Again Miss West makes Miss Melville so absurdly squeamish that we wonder whether she is not merely using her for an argument for more sexual knowledge for young women. This may be so, but why on earth does Miss West let Miss Melville be a member of the feminist movement, the leaders of that highly intellectual body would never permit in their ranks such a stupid prudish and utterly contemptible young person as Miss Melville. Miss West seems to know very little about feminism, if she thinks that it can be helped by women who think babies are the effect of an embrace, the increase in the birth rate if such was the case would be phenomenal. Here is a picture of the timid Miss Melville desiring to know about babies and terrified to learn.

" She had laid her fingers between its leaves, but a shivering had come upon her, and she ran downstairs very quickly and washed her hands."

.   .   .   .

I am rather afraid that Miss West has a certain contempt
for bank clerks.   After all they are quite harmless people,
they do not sit on a stool from choice but a country without banks would be a little peculiar.   The dialogue (and
Miss West can write quite good dialogue) between Yaverland and Ellen's mother shows a rather superior attitude
to bank clerks, a little unfair for they are really nice men
and live very blameless lives in very blameless villas.

> " ' I like a man to travel,' she went on, tossing her head
> and looking altogether fierce Ellen's mother.   ' I never
> go into the bank without looking at the clerks and
> thinking what sumphs they are, sitting on their high
> stools.' "

Miss West has a splendid description of the lust of
dancing.   It is admirable that she should state so plainly
that the attraction of dancing is a pandering to sexual
lust.   Of course it is.   It must be little disturbing
to high minded curates who organise dances in aid of the
further glory of God, to realise, if they ponder deeply
enough, that they are helping prostitution and en
couraging adultery.   There is no more revolting spectacle
than a number of men and women rubbing bodies together
in aid of a Church, while the pleasant vicar and the genial
curate watch the spectacle and gloat over the fact that
twenty more pounds has been collected to repair the
squeaking organ or the leaking roof.

> " By nothing more than a thin wall which shook to
> music was this little home divided from a thick aired
> place where ugly people lurched against each other
> lustfully."

At times Miss West is uncanny in her perception, but it is nasty reading for perfectly magnanimous mothers who take their perfectly innocent daughters to dances, to know that the seeds being sown are lust and licence.

Probably because she can probe so deeply into human conduct is a reason that makes Miss West rather angry with humanity. While the ability to probe deeply into human nature may reveal that humanity is really good, the reverse can also be quite easily ascertained, that humanity is bad, honest on account of fear, hypocritical and unsound. The mistake that Miss West seems to make is that she sees the bad side of humanity and fails to see the other. This is in marked contrast to Mr. Maxwell, who has the unusual ability for seeing both sides. But then Miss West is a comparatively new comer to fiction and Mr. Maxwell is a very old and accomplished writer of novels.

If of course you are championing an unpopular cause, you may expect to think that people are unpleasant, for they will not smile at you but frown and sneer. Miss West in " The Judge " does champion the cause of feminism and at present feminism is not popular with the masses, it is distrusted by the average woman, for the average woman still prefers a baby to a vote, it is disliked by men, for the more successful is feminism, the more dangerous rivals will women become.

It is sometimes a little difficult to imagine that Miss West has her " human " side, her side when she is away from screeching political women, needed reforms for women and violent tirades against men-made laws and all the conditions of civilisation which women wish to alter, yet do not seem able to make laws mucn better. It is pleasant to record a piece of dialogue between Yaverland

and Miss Melville, which is the type of conversation which
always takes place between men and women, when the
interest of the moment is themselves. It is pleasing to
find Miss West a little unbending and not quite so cross,
able to write of the glory that is love slowly being born,
able to appreciate that embryo lovers do not talk feminism ethics, but simple barbaric and delightful nonsense.
Here is a delicious picture of Yaverland talking to Ellen
and in the distance there comes a small sound, and it must
be the murmur of hearts that proceeds the kiss.

" ' Your pockets are like a boy's,' he said. ' In a way
you're awfully like a boy.'
" I wish I was,' she answered bitterly. ' But I'm
a girl, and I've nothing before me. No going to sea
for me as there was for you.' "

A most unexpected and peculiar writer is Miss West, she
can write really wonderfully concerning the effect of a kiss
on a young woman like Miss Melville. The dualism of
pain and pleasure produced by the physical contact is
splendidly written. The gradual evolution to a sensation
of love, caused by kissing is a fine piece of psychology, for
a kiss not only touches the lips, it thrusts through to the
brain and smothers all, except the intoxication of loving.

" A pervading weakness fell on her ; her arms, which
had somehow become linked round his neck, were now
as soft as garlands, her knees failed under her shivering
body : but through her mind thundered grandiose
convictions of new power. There was no sea, black
with chill and depth, in which she would not die to
save him, no desert whose unwatered sands she would
not travel if so she served his need."

So Miss West pilots us through the raging storm, the terrific flood of emotions and we come suddenly sailing gently into the calm waters and the anchor is weighed for the harbour is the harbour of love.

" Love began to travel over her body, lighting here and there little fires of ecstasy, making her adore him with her skin as she had always adored him with her heart."

Perhaps we are more prone to misinterpret the probable wishes of the dead than the living. We put on black for a person we know quite well hated any kind of ostentation on his behalf, we cease from social activities and think we are paying tribute to someone who dies after a full life in every way. Supposing the dead do know what we do and the supposition is quite reasonable for we are agreed that knowledge is a spiritual energy, it must be a little irritating to them to see the inane way that we endeavour to give them respect. As a matter of fact the only respect that should be given to the dead is to leave them alone, neither paint their blackness blacker or their whiteness more white. This is of course the one thing we never do, we imagine that death turns a villain into a saint, or when he has been dead sufficiently long enough, we turn round and discover that he led a horrible life and enterprising people write biographies of long dead people and there is born a new personality, that never by any chance was the real individual. All of which gets me back again to Miss West, for I think that she demands that the dead be treated rationally, that they be treated more or less as if they were still physically alive. If, of course, it be argued that the dead are really so dead that they are no longer existing anywhere, then we can say what we like for they cannot know.

But most people who pursue their life, as though the trend of it must be influenced by some dead person, assume, whether they are conscious of it or not, some very definite belief in immortality.

Miss West by means of two or three lines of dialogue puts forward a very sensible position with regard to considering wishes of dead persons or rather what we think would be their wishes if they could be expressed. I would of course say in passing that Spiritualism declares that the actual wishes of dead persons *can* be expressed by them, but at present it must be recognised that Spiritualism is but a movement and I do not consider that it has so proved immortality that there is no longer any doubt about it. The dialogue concerns the question of marriage soon after the death of a parent. The problem is whether the marriage should be indefinitely postponed in deference to the memory of a mother. Let Miss West state her own position.

" ' Ellen, when will you marry Richard ?'
" ' We've talked it over,' said Ellen, with a certain solemn fear. 'We think we'll wait Six months. Out of respect for mother.' "

Then Miss West introduces her fine retort and the retort in my opinion demonstrates an admirable philosophy of respect to the dead and what they would have we who are still alive, do.

" ' But, my dear, your mother won't get any pleasure out of Richard being kept waiting. She'd like you to settle down and be happy.' "

This surely shows a very sound judgment on the part
of Miss West and a very human one as well.

.   .   .   .

It is perhaps rather natural that having said a good deal
about death we should go to the other extreme and say
something about birth. For some obscure reason Miss
West is not nearly so sound when she talks about birth
as when she ruminates on death. Her writing about
death is really fine and in no way objectionable, her
writing about birth is sickening and has no acute perception whatever. Miss Melville imagining what birth really
is like is deplorable and Miss West's interpretation is
equally deplorable. I will give a quotation to show how
Miss West wallows in the uninteresting details of birth,
details which have no need in fiction whatever, even when
written by very skilful novelists, and when written by
Miss West in her evident immaturity, execrable.

" Even yet she was not clear concerning the processes
of birth. But in her mind's eye she saw Marion lying on
a narrow bed, her body clenched under the blankets,
and her face pale and concave at cheek and temple with
sickness and persecuted resolution, holding at bay with
her will a crowd of doctors pressing round her with
scalpels in their hands, preserving by her tensity the
miracle of life that was to be Richard."

There is nothing subtle about this, it is mere physical
description and makes out that birth is a loathsome un-
wished for thing, instead of the most natural, if the most
painful process in the world. But perhaps this book
" The Judge " is mainly written for women, if so they

REBECCA WEST

will no doubt love to gloat over Miss West's morbid tendencies, they will no doubt feel that she is on their side that she is the champion of oppressed woman, but Miss West is writing a novel, not a medical treatise or a feminist pamphlet.

" The Judge " depicts a writer of tremendous possibilities and a very fair achievement. Miss West is a little too convinced of her own point of view to make a really great novelist. Her outlook is too pessimistic to produce the healthy romantic novel which is so wanted in our own time. At times she rises to very great heights indeed, her actual literary work is excellent and her thought is reasonable. At others she sinks to a very mediocre achievement and her thought is unpleasant and really might easily be the grousings of a disappointed woman.

" The Judge " rightly enough in spite of some of its weaknesses received a great deal of attention and but little hostility when it was published. Though it is no part of this book to say anything about Miss West's study of Henry James it must be conceded that there is a good deal to suggest that she is a far better critic than a novelist. Possibly she is too sound a critic to be a really first class novelist ! All the time through the story contained in " The Judge " we feel that Miss West is not primarily telling a story but is criticising certain social condition and demanding that more power be given to women. There is no need to quarrel with this Ethic, but it has to be remembered that a large number of people even to-day expect to find a story when they find a novel and demand a good story rather than a good essay under the guise of fiction.

Miss West has as yet given but a small quantity of literature to the world. In many ways what she has given has shown a mixture of brilliant and superficial qualities.

.   .   .   .

If Miss West cultivates a more optimistic outlook, a keener sense of the fact that humanity is neither all good or all bad but a little of each, she will probably produce better and more agreeable work. " The Judge " in the opinion of the writer of this book, full of admirable writing and thought as it is, is distinctly marred by the suggestion all through that the writer, is pessimistic, bitter and inclined to think the unfortunate and much tried people of the world but "a little breed." Miss West may be right, but she will give us better work, if she does not miss the potential goodness this world contains.

In a word Miss West has achieved much, but she gives the clearest indications that she could achieve so much more.

END OF PORTRAIT SEVEN